Back country poems

Sam Walter Foss

Contents

BACK COUNTRY POEMS

BY

Sam Walter Foss

BACK COUNTRY POEMS,

THE VOLUNTEER ORGANIST.

THE gret big church wuz crowded full uv broadcloth an U uv silk,
An' satins rich as cream thet grows on our ol' brindle's milk;
Shined boots, biled shirts, stiff dickeys, an stove-pipe hats were there,
An' doods 'ith trouserloons so tight they couldn' kneel in prayer.

The elder in his poolpit high, said, as he slowly riz:
" Our organist is kep' to hum, laid up 'ith roomatiz,
An as we hev no substitoot, as brother Moore ain't here,
Will some un in. the congergation be so kind 's to volunteer? "

An' then a red-nosed, drunken tramp, of low-toned, rowdy style,
Give an interduct'ry hiccup, an' then staggered up the aisle;
Then thro' the holy atmosphere there crep' a sense er sin,
An' thro' thet air er sanctity the odor uv ol' gin.

Then Deacon Purin'ton he yelled, his teeth all sot on edge
" This man purfanes the house er God ! W'y, this is sakerlege
The tramp didn' hear a word he said, but slouched 'I stumblin' feet,
An' sprawled an' staggered up the steps, an' gained the org;
seat.

He then went pawrin' thro' the keys, an' soon there riz strain

Thet seemed to jest bulge out the heart, an Mectrify the brail
An then he slapped down on the thing ith hands an he; an' knees,—
He slam-dashed his hull body down kerflop upon the keys.

The organ roared, the music flood went sweepin high an di
It swelled into the rafters, an' bulged out into the sky,
The ol' church shook an' staggered, an seemed to reel a sway,
An the elder shouted " Glory !" an' I yelled out " Hooray

An then he tried a tender strain thet melted in our ears,
Thet brought up blessed memories an drenched 'em do' 'ith tears;
An' we dreamed uv ol' time kitchens, 4th Tabby on the ma
Uv home an luv an baby days, an mother, an' all that!

An' then he struck a streak uv hope — a song from sou forgiven —
Thet burst from prison-bars uv sin, an' stormed the gates heaven;
The mornin' stars they sung together, — no soul wuz alone, —
We felt the universe wuz safe, an God wuz on his throne !

An' then a wail uv deep despair an' darkness come again,
An long black crape hung on the doors uv all the homes uv men;
No luv, no light, no joy, no hope, no songs uv glad delight,—
An' then the tramp, he staggered down an reeled into the night!

But we knew he'd tol' his story, though he never spoke a
word, An' it wuz the saddest story thet our ears hed ever heard;
He hed tol' his own life history, an no eye wuz dry thet day,
Wen the elder rose an' simply said: " My brethren, let us pray."

THE UNCANOONUC MOUNTAINS.

THEY stood there in the distance, mysterious and lone,
Each with a hazy vapor above its towering dome;

They stood like barriers between the unknown and the known,
The Uncanoonuc Mountains which I used to see from home.
And far beyond the mountains, I was told, the world was wide,
And in fancy on the thither side it was my wont to roam;
I saw the glories of the world upon the other side
Of the Uncanoonuc Mountains which I used to see from home.

On this side the Uncanoonucs was an old, familiar scene;
But *they* were burnished pillars on which rainbows used to rest;
On this side the Uncanoonucs all was commonplace and mean;
They were red with sunset splendor at the threshold of the West.
They were Mountains of Enchantment that stood guard at the frontier
Of the Borderland of Mystery, bathed in twilight's crimson foam.
And I longed to reach their summits, and pass on without a fear,
Through the Uncanoonuc Mountains which I used to see from home.
I have passed the Uncanoonucs, and have travelled far away
Through the Borderland of Mystery upon an endless quest;
But other Uncanoonucs, glimmering in the twilight gray,
Still lift their hazy summits at the threshold of the West.

One misty mountain overpassed upon the march of time,
Another summit breaks in view, and onward still I roam —
Another mountain in the mist which beckons me to climb,
Like the Uncanoonuc Mountains which I used to see from home.

Though beyond the Uncanoonucs all the glories that I seek
Fail to fashion to realities before my wistful eyes,
I still will chase the Vision—see her standing on the peak
Of that other Uncanoonuc towering in the western skies.
I grasp my mountain-climbing staff—there yet is ample time —
For some other Uncanoonuc ever lifts its distant dome —
With my boyhood faith I'll climb it, as I used to long to climb
The Uncanoonuc Mountains which I used to see from home.

THE RAILROAD THROUGH THE FARM.

THERE'S thet black abomernation, thet big locomotiv there,
Its smoke-tail like a pirut flag, a-wavin through the ail An'
I mus' set, twelve times a day, an' never raise my arm,
An' see thet gret black monster go a-snortin' through m farm.

My father's farm, my grandsir's farm, — I come of Pilgril stock —
My great-great-great-great-grandsir's farm, way back t Plymouth Rock;
Way back in the sixteen hundreds it was in our family name
An' no man dared to trespass till that tootin' railroad came.

I sez, "You can't go through this farm, you hear it flat al plain!"
An' then they blabbed about the right of " eminunt domain. "
Who's Eminunt Domain? " sez I, "I want you folks to see
Thet on this farm there ain't no man so eminunt ez me."

An' w'en their gangs begun to dig I went out with a gun,
An' they rushed me off to prison till their wretched woi wuz done.
" If I can't purtect my farm," sez I, " w'y, then, it's my idc
You'd better shet off callin' this ' the country of the free.' "

There, there, ye hear it toot agin an' break the peaceful caln
I tell ye, you black monster, you've no business on my farm
An' men ride by in stovepipe hats, an' women loll in silk,
An', lookin' in my barnyard, say, " See thet ol codger milk !

Git off my farm, you stuck-up doods, who set in there an' grin,
I own this farm, railroad an' all, an' I will fence it in!
Ding-ding, toot-toot, you black ol fiend, you'll find w'en you come back,
An *ol'* rail fence, without no bars, built straight across the track.

An' then you stuck-up doods inside, you Pullman upper crust,
Will know this codger'll hold his farm an' let the railroad bust.
You'll find this railroad all fenced in — 'twon't do no good to talk —
If you want to git to Boston, w'y jest take yer laigs an' walk.

THE GRAVE WITHIN THE GLEN.

DOWN in a wild vine tangled glen
Young Herman lived, remote from men.
The silence of the ancient hills
Kept guard around the lonely vale,
Unbroken but by laughing rills
And sad songs of the nightingale.
Thus, bright with morning's crimson glow,
His life was free and all his own,
But, like a brook beneath the snow,
Flowed on unnoted and unknown.

Then came the rainbow dream of feme —
The world's applause for righted wrongs,
The glory of a sounding name,
A grateful nation's loud acclaim,
And mighty poets' plausive songs.
To win the meed of human praise
He vowed to dedicate his days—
To gain the cheers of listening throngs,
To shine the victor of debate,
To shape the councils of the state,
Or make men love him for his songs.

He climbed the valley's beetling walls
To seek the praise of foolish men,
And left the rainbowed waterfalls

And sunset glories of the Glen.
Young Herman found the way was long-
No poet cheered him with his song,
And for the thunder trump of fame,
To bruit abroad his wide-flown name,
He heard the hisses of the throng,
And loud and bitter jeers of shame.

The hoary wrong that sapped the state,
By age and form grown venerate,
Hurled back the arrows of his hate.
The creed he hunted to its death,
That built its shrines on human fears,
Its altars wet with human tears,
Reviled him with its dying breath.
And Error, throned in regal state,
From out her storehouse of the past,
At him in wrathful menace cast
Her wealth of immemorial hate.

And while his foot was on her neck,
She flung at him her poisoned dart,
The bitter name that rankles sore :
He wore it, bleeding, in his heart, —
The grand old name of heretic,
That all the martyrs bore.
Instead of words of human praise
To cheer and light his stormy days,
Like mists from off a stagnant fen
Came curses from the hearts of men.
Then deadlier hate from hate was born,
He gave his mockers scorn for scorn;
His days were battles, and his life

Grew weary of the unequal strife.
He sought his mountain-guarded glen
To die in peace, remote from men;
And through the gates of solitude,
Where death's dark shadows overbrood,
Leaving his purposed work unwrought,
He found the silence that he sought.

So, while the mournful nightingale
Filled with her dirge the solemn vale,
His worn, world-weary form found rest
In the deep valley's flowery breast.
But the stern deeds that he had done
Remained and worked their perfect will ;
And time was faithful to fulfil
The work he purposed 'neath the sun;
And the lone grave within the Glen,
Of him despised and feared of men,
Became the shrine of saint and sage,
The patriot's boast, a nation's pride,
The goal of loving pilgrimage,
By song and story glorified.

But Fame breathed forth her votive breath
On unresponsive lips of death,
The chaplet crown of laggard
Fate Pressed on the pulseless brow too late.

BOBOLINK PHILOSOPHY.

I KNOW a deep philosopher who's far too wise to think,
That bubbling, breezy blatherskite, the boisterous bobo link.
So drunk is he with wine of joy, so music-mad with mirth,

His tipsy carols of content rejuvenate the earth.

We feel the orient joy of life with which our world began—
'Tis summer in the earth and air and in the heart of man.
From what deep fount of flowing joy does this mad minstrel drink,
This babbling, breezy blatherskite, this boisterous bobolink ?

From rounded apple-blossom cups where wild bees browse and boom;
From tiger-lily beakers, and from chalices of bloom ;
From strawberry goblets filled with dew, the incense of the night,
Caught from the sky's inverted urn embossed with starry light.

Forth from his blossom bed he leaps, and, laughingly and strong,
All up and down the ringing earth he weaves his web of song,

And preaches boldly to the sad the folly of despair,
And tells to whom it may concern that all the world is fair.

And to my heart his wisdom finds a surer welcome home
Than some that has been sanctioned by the sages of old Rome.

That bubbling, breezy blatherskite, the boisterous bobolink,
Is such a deep philosopher, he's far too wise to think.

THE TOLLBRIDGE KEEPER.

I LIVE here by my tollbridge
Content, without a want,—
My bridge, that joins these mighty States,
New Hampshire and Vermont.
The big Connecticut below
Among its piers is whirled;
I'm acquainted with the river

That's acquainted with the world.

For it goes winding on and on,
Through bowlders, hills, and sand,
A crinkly silver watch chain
On the jacket of the land.
And, though I live here all alone
Within my cottage curled,
I'm acquainted with the river
That's acquainted with the world.

Through maple-sugar orchards,
And through the fields of hay,
And down through the tobacco farms
It winds upon its way;
And it sleeps in silent meadows
When the twilight settles down,
Then winds its cool, soft arm around
The hot brows of the town.

The people on the other side,
It is their only care
To cross to this, while people here
All wish to cross to there;
And after pondering long,
I think That, though the world is wide,
I am the only man on earth
Who's wholly satisfied.

And why should I not be content?
I sit here evermore,
While all the world to humor me
Goes riding by my door.

And when the latest wheel at night
Across the bridge is whirled,
I'm acquainted with the river
That's acquainted with the world,

"Why does my river hurry so?
What can its errand be?"
And it says, " I hear the music,
Hear the anthem of the sea."
"Stay and talk to me of cities
Where the many thousands be,
" But it says, " I feel the magic
Of the music of the sea."

Well I know the truth, my river,
That thou sayest unto me,
For I, too, have felt the magic
Of the music of the sea.
Though I live far in the mountains,
Still the Stream of Life is whirled
Toward the mist-enshrouded ocean
That encircles all the world.

THE ROAD TO BOSTON.

THE little road goes past my house, goes winding like a snake,
Climbs up the hills of hemlock, and winds through swamps of brake,
It leaps the sweeping river and climbs the mountain height,
Bends down into the valley, and goes glimmering out of sight.

But there are travellers tell me that the little road grows wide,
And leads through many villages down to the ocean side,
And still keeps stretching onward — they have followed day by day —

Until it reaches Boston town, two hundred miles away.
And this little road, they tell me, grows to Boston's biggest street,
All lined by mighty houses tall—and some two hundred feet —
Where monstrous crowds its sidewalks throng, like armies on parade;
Where all the people of the world come down to buy and trade.

My boys and girls when they grew up, they felt the heavy load
Of this quietude and dulness — and they travelled down the road,
And they wound across the rivers, and far o'er the mountains gray,
To the biggest street in Boston, two hundred miles away.

And many men among the hills hear Boston's distant roar,
For the biggest street in Boston passes every farmhouse door,
And the distant roar and rumble comes like magic to the ear,
And thousands travel down the road, pass on, and disappear.

But my boys they write from Boston that, for feet that waded through
The early fields of clover and the daisies and the dew,
The stones are hard and cruel there on Boston's biggest street,
And are pressed each day and hour by a horde of tired feet.

And that men are cold and selfish, each one busy with his plan
To climb to wealth and power o'er his prostrate fellow-man;
That the few have ease and comfort, and the many toil and die,
Shut in by brick and granite from the sunlight and the sky.

And I write my children letters; tell them that their father still,
Still is toiling by the roadside on the green and quiet hill,
And to come away from Boston, with its cruel noise and roar,
For the biggest street in Boston passes by their father's door!

W'EN MELINDY TOL' ME "YES".

JEST a fortni't from my fall-out with my first sweetheart, Lucindy,
Did Melindy, my Melindy, tell me "Yes";
And the atmosphere was windy, way from Pokumville to Indy
Windy with the breezy music of etarnal blessedness.
An' she said it fair an' squarely, an' not " Call again,"
" May be," An' a New Jerusalum glory lit the fiel' an' wilderness,
An' the sun bust out like laughter on the round face of a baby,
Wen Melindy, my Melindy, tol' me "Yes !"

Like a twenty-million orchestra away beyon' all counting,
' The bob'links bubbled over in a music waterfall;
An' I felt just like a-mountin' on the meetin' house an' shoutin',
That Paradise was open, with admission free to all.

Each grass blade in the medder was a string to Natur's fiddle,
Thet wuz played on by the zephyrs with a velvety caress;
An' OF Natur's jints were limbered, an' she shashayed down the middle,
W'en Melindy, my Melindy, tol' me " Yes ! "

An' the angels played so bully, thet the music reached the gateway,
An' came spillin' through the op'in' an' a-singing down to earth, —
Came a-singin' such a great way thet the universe wuz straightway
Shoutn' in the glad redem'tion of a holy secon' birth; An' I —
I set a-straddle on the ridge-pole of Creation,
An' only fit to holler in my hootin' happiness,
Wen Melindy, my Melindy, filled my heart 'ith jubilation,
Wen Melindy, my Melindy, tol' *me* " Yes !"

NEW YEAR RIGHTEOUSNESS.

ABOUT New Year's I grit my teeth, I brace my feet an' swear
Thet I'll rastle with ol' Satan an' down him every¬where ;
A fittin' chum for Baxter's saints, a man of heavenly worth,
An angel with red whiskers, I will roam about the earth.

So I make a lunge for Satan, who Stan's a-leerin' there,
An' plant my right fist on his nose, my left han' in his hair;
An' he staggers like a drunken man, an' totters, with a groan—
The frien' of sin, the foe of man, he lies there overthrown

An' so, on January first, 'neath Virtue's soft caress,
I feel all soaked in sanctity, an' steeped in righteousness,
A sort er walkin' meetin'-house, all sin-born fears are fled—
For, don't the righteous own the earth, an' ain't the devil dead?

But the day after New Year's Day, the devil moves his head,
An' I am all broke up to find the old scamp isn't dead;
An' later in the afternoon, he jest begins to blink,
An' has the cheek to lift his head, 'an cock his eye an' wink.

An' then on January third he starts to limp about,
An' I walk up an' say to him: "I'm glad to see you out."
An' then he jest hol's out his han' for me to come an' take it,
An' I, like a big, tarnal fool, jest waltz right up and shake it.

These little New Year's battles Satan thinks is only play,
If you want to worst the devil, you must trounce him every day;
So, every day, jest grit yer teeth, an' brace yer feet, an' swear
That you'll rastle with ol' Satan, an' down him everywhere !

THE PATH THROUGH THE WOOD.

W'EN I was a kid I driv' the cows to parsture every day,
An' I'd go and fetch 'em home at night, and think it on'y play:
But sometimes, arter dark come on, where the black ol' hemlocks stood,
I'd git so sca't that I would fly through the long, long path through the wood.
'Twas a long, long path through the wood,
An' I tell yeou,
That I jest flew
Through the long, long path through the wood.

I skipped along by the open fiel', an' danced an' scampered an' sung,
An' whistled a toon thet jest kep' time with the toon the cowbells rung.
An' Brindle an' Whiteface 'ud frolic an' scoot— seemed 's if they understood
—
Until we come to the aidge of the swamp, an' the long, long path through the
wood.
My ! the long, long path through the wood;
It was crowded with hosts
Of critters an' ghosts,
That long, long path through the wood.

But 'tain't on'y boys thet drive their cows, but men in country and town,
Thet travel a path thet is thick 'ith fears, long arter the sun goes down;
For many a man has trembled and shook, where the dark, black hemlocks
stood,
Has shook at the ghosts of his own dead days, in his long, long path through
the wood.
Tis a long, long path through the wood,
With a dew of tears
From the long gone years,
Oh, the long, long path through the wood.

An' there ain't no feet, as I un'erstan', but mus' travel the path some day,
Wen the big sun sinks behin' the hills, an' the worl' grows col' an' gray;
For we all git lost in the hemlock hills, where the big black shadders brood,
An' are chased by the ghosts of turribul fears, through the long, long path through the wood.
Ah, the long, long path through the wood,
Through the path er dread
Thet all must tread,
The long, long path through the wood.

Yes, we all hev to walk through the hemlock path, through the path that stretches far,
Wen the silence er darkness comes down on the soul, an' the midnight has no star;
An' we fight in the awful dark alone, as strong an' brave men should,
But there's scars on the soul w'en it comes at last through the long, long path through the wood;
Ah, the long, long path through the wood,
An' scars thet will stay
Till its dyin' day, —
Oh, the long, long path through the wood.

JIM'S FUTURE.

JIM has a future front of him," —
J That's what they used to say of Jim,
For when young Jim was only ten
He mingled with the wisest men, —
With wisest men he used to mix,
And talk of law and politics;
And everybody said of Jim,
" He has a future front of him."

When Jim was twenty years of age,
All costumed, ready for life's stage,
He had a perfect man's physique,
And knew philosophy and Greek;
He'd delved in every misty tome
Of old Arabia and Rome;
And everybody said of Jim,
" He has a future front of him."

When Jim was thirty years of age,
He'd made a world-wide pilgrimage,
He'd walked and studied 'neath the trees,
Of German universities,
And visited and pondered on
The sites of Thebes and Babylon;
And everybody said of Jim,
" He has a future front of him." .

The heir to all earth's heritage,
Was Jim at forty years of age,
The lore of all the years was shut,
And focussed in his occiput;
And people thought, so much he knew,
" What wondrous things our Jim will do ! "
They more than ever said of Jim,
" He has a future front of him."

At fifty years, though Jim was changed,
He had his knowledge well arranged,
All tabulated, systemized,
And adequately synthesized.
His head was so well filled within,

He thought: " I'm ready to begin.
" And everybody said of Jim, "
He has a future front of him."

At sixty — no more need be said —
At sixty years poor Jim was dead.
The preacher said that such as he
Would shine to all eternity;
In other worlds, beyond the blue,
There was great work for Jim to do;
And o'er his bier he said of Jim,
" He has a future front of him."

The great deeds we are going to do
Shine 'gainst the vastness of the blue,
Like sunset clouds of lurid light
Against the background of the night;
And so we climb the endless slope,
Far up the crownless heights of hope;
And each one makes himself a Jim,
And rears a future front of him.

A CHILD'S QUESTION.

W HEN the fragrant breeze was loaded with perfume,
When the joyous Maytime season, bright and fair,
Arrayed herself in robes of bud and bloom,
And a storm of apple blossoms filled the air —
Then I watched a sturdy father in his prime
Bending low, his little daughter's voice to hear:
" Why don't the birds sing, father, all the time,
And the apple blossoms blossom all the year? "

" Ah," thought I, " were all as sweet and pure and good
As this sunny little maid with golden hair,
Our lives would have no wintry solitude —
It would be summer always, everywhere.
We would live in an eternal flower clime,
And the storm that breaks in thunder none would fear,
For the song birds would be with us all the time,

And the apple blossoms blossom all the year."

PATHS.

THE path that leads to a Loaf of Bread
Winds through the Swamps of Toil,
And the path that leads to a Suit of Clothes
Goes through a flowerless soil,
And the paths that lead to a Loaf of Bread.
And the Suit of Clothes are hard to tread.

And the path that leads to a House of Your Own
Climbs over the bowldered hills,
And the path that leads to a Bank Account
Is swept by the blast that kills:
But the men who start in the paths to-day
In the Lazy Hills may go astray.

In the Lazy Hills are trees of shade,
By the dreamy Brooks of Sleep,
And the rollicking River of Pleasure laughs,
And gambols down the steep;
But when the blasts of Winter come,
The brooks and the river are frozen dumb.
Then woe to those in the Lazy Hills

When the blasts of Winter moan,
Who strayed from the path to a Bank Account
And the path to a House of Their Own;
These paths are hard in the summer heat,
But in Winter they lead to a snug retreat.

THE MILKING OF THE COW.

THE milk pail used to versify a mild and mellow metre,
When I used to milk old Brindle in the yard,
And the shining milk was sweeter unto me and little Peter
Than oriental perfumes of frankincense and nard,
The sunset flung its banners from the gilded hills about us,
And the odors of the evening seemed to drop from every bough,
There was peace and glad contentment both within us and without us,
At the sweet mellifluous milking of the cow.

And wandering, like a memory from the silent past's abysm,
I smell the grateful odors of the fragrant evening breeze,
And I bend to catch the chrism of the twilight's glad baptism,
And the outstretched benediction of the trees.
The glory of the summer night, the magic of the mountains,
And the tinklings of the twilight on the form are with me now,
But through all the mingling music still I hear those falling fountains,
The sweet mellifluous milking of the cow.

Still I hear the joyful rhythm of that titillating tinkle,
And I smell the grateful odors of the placid, perfumed night,—
Odors blown from glens a-sprinkle with wild-rose and peri-winkle,
And from lakes where lazy lilies loll in languor for the light.

Through the valley of the Long Years that is glimmering behind me
I peer adown the vista that connects the then and now,

With a youth's audacious unconcern a careless boy I find me,
At the sweet mellifluous milking of the cow.

MEMORIAL DAY.

DNOT as white saints without a blot,
Whose souls were stainless of a spot
Were these plain men of average cla
But mortal, like plain men to-day.
For always, in dark hours of need,
A man is furnished for the deed;
And always when the storm clouds lower,
Strong men are ready for the hour.
And thus, from earth's most common breed
Spring heroes fit for every need.

These men were common men, 'tis true,
Just common men like me and you.
The plain man is the basic clod
From which we grow the demigod;
And in the average man is curled
The hero stuff that rules the world.
And so we deck, on hill and glen,
The hero graves of common men.

Plain, common men of every day,
Who left their homes to march away,
To perish on the battle plain,
As common men will do again;
To lift a ghastly, glazing eye
Up to a lurid stranger sky
Until it sees a painted rag —
The same old common spangled flag —

And then to die, and testify
To all the ages, far and nigh,
How commonplace it is to die.

It is not merely now and then
We find such hearts in common men, —
Such hero souls enwrapt away
In swathing folds of common clay —
But standing face to face with fate,
All common men are always great.
For men are cowards in the gloom
Of their own little, selfish fears, —
Not when the thunder-steps of doom
Stride through the trembling years.
And in an open fight with fate
All common men are always great.

THE BURSTING OF THE BOOM.

OUR village was the boomingest rip-roaring place you ever sawn,
An alder swamp, in thirty days, would grow into a public lawn,
Scrub parstures grew to public parks, and frog ponds into trim front yards,
An' fox trails into public streets, an' cow paths into boolevards !

We had a libr'y an' high skule, two letter carriers for the mail,
Four churches with four choir rows, two lawyers, an' a bang-up jail,
Two editers who fit in style no New York editer could beat,—
One had " a vile an' scurrilous rag," an* one " a low an' measly sheet."

"What made the town die out?" you ask. It was the strangest thing, I swear, —
Smith's dog chased Eben Johnson's cat, an' that's the whole of the affair.
An' Johnson said Smith set him on, an' Smith said Johnson was a liar,
So Johnson set the flame agoin', an' Smith poured ile upon the fire.

Then Mrs. Smith perked up her nose at Mrs. Johnson in the street,
The little Johnsonses an' Smiths wouldn't speak at all if they should meet;
The sewing circle then took sides an' soon broke up in wordy fights,
For part took sides with Mrs. Smith, an' part were Johnsonites.

The trouble got into the church, an' then, instid o' praise an' prayer,
The pastor got his fingers mixed in Deacon Peleg Putnam's hair;
The prayer-meet'n broke up in noise; next day the minister resigned,
An' Deacon Putnam he went roun' with one eye black an' t'other blind.

Young Smithites courtin' Johnsonites, broke off with their purspective brides,
An' soon there was two lunatics an' then three suicides;
Then half the young men moved from town, an' soon were followed by their pals,
For what is life but jest a bore to bright young men without no gals!
Folks moved away, the stores failed up, the bottom dropped out of the boom,
The bank it busted, an' we thought nex' thing we'd hear the crack of doom.
An' now the grass grows in our streets, an' the whole boom has fallen flat;
But Johnson's cat an' Smith's old dog are doin' well an' growin' fat !

THE CARVEN NAME.

I WANDERED in the forest, when
My sated soul had tired of men,
Till to a spreading beech I came,
And on it idly carved my name;
Then lightly threw myself across
A forest-couch of fragrant moss,
Where soon I sank in slumber deep
And softly entered, through the gleam
Of misty porticos of Sleep,
The shadowy Palace of a Dream.

I dreamed how through the years would grow,
Alternate clothed with leaves and snow,
Through April's tears, October's flame,
The beech-tree with the carven name;
And bird and squirrel overhead
Peer down upon my name unread,
While Solitude, upon his throne,
Would reign in silence o'er his own,
Until some hunter with his gun,
O'erwearied by the noonday sun,
Companioned by his panting dog,
Would seat him on some mossy log,
And, glancing up, a glad surprise —
My carven name — would meet his eyes;
And he would see before him wrought
The symbol of a vanished thought,
A silent influence to bind
A severed being to his kind.

Then changed the scene, the years glide on,
A quarter-century has gone.
Tis Morn in Winter; o'er the snows
The sturdy woodman taskward goes.
The ground with fallen trunks he strews,
And down the forest avenues
The echoes of his axe are heard
By startled hare and wondering bird.
New comrades join him, day by day,
And bravely hew their onward way;
In the keen air their axes glance,
And chime, as to the wood-nymph's dance;
The music of the cross-cut saw

Breaks through the wood's cathedral awe,
And Solitude, spoiled of his own,
Goes forth to seek another throne.
But soon the patient woodmen reach,
And pause beneath, the ancient beech;
Then, in a backwoods parle, decide
To leave the monarch in his pride;
For all unite with one acclaim
To spare it for the stranger's name.

Again a change: before mine eye
There sways a shimmering plain of rye,
And the winds, raving wild and free,
Toss it, in billows, like the sea.
But, in the midst of ripened sheaves,
The old beech wears its crown of leaves;
In Autumn's regal glory stands,
The hierarch of the harvest lands:
And weary laborers are laid
In noonday rest beneath its shade.
The carven name their curious eyes
Question with many a vague surmise;
Till an old man with locks of snow
Tells how a dreamer, long ago,
First carved the name in idling mood In
Nature's untrod solitude.
And strange unto their fancy seems
This dreamer from a land of dreams,
Whose life, unknown for praise or blame,
Had left no record but his name.

The vision widens: on mine eye
No longer waves the ripened rye;

But lo ! within a play-ground neat
The schoolhouse of a village street.
The ancient beech before it stands,
Waving abroad yet mightier hands;
And darting warblers from the tree
Pour down their madrigals of glee.
Beneath, the children at their play
Are glad, are jubilant as they.
Ah ! long shall memory recall
This daily school-boy carnival!
To men and matrons, old and gray,
This sport shall seem but yesterday.
For memory casts a rainbow screen
Around the years that intervene.
And so the craggy heights of age
Look down directly on the smooth
Green vales of childhood's heritage —
The dewy meadow-lands of youth !

The schoolboy with his favorite maid
Lingers beneath the ancient shade,
And feels a rapture which the years
With all their laughter and their tears
Can from his memory ne'er remove, —
The rapture of an earliest love !
Dream on beneath the beechen shade,
Gay barefoot boy and laughing maid;
Dream on, nor soon awake to see
Life's stern and cold reality, —
Its tender buds of promise killed,
Its morning visions unfulfilled;
Dream on, nor soon awake to learn
That dead loves never more return !

The vision heightens: I behold,
With silvery spires and domes of gold
Far, far beyond my dazzled eyes,
A city towering to the skies;
And standing 'mid the din and glare
Of traffic's thronging thoroughfare,
The same old carven beech looks down
On all the tumult of the town.
And hurrying merchants pause to mark
The moss-grown letters on its bark;
For many a legend, strange and fair,
And many a story, old and rare,
And tale and song and minstrelsy
Have glorified the ancient tree.
It links the city's swarming brood
With nature's pathless solitude;
And joins an age of bard and sage
With olden ages, coarse and rude.

But see ! a light breeze from the farms
Has caught the old tree in its arms;
It falls, and round it in a ring
Men swarm, as fiefs around a king
Who, of life's pageant weary grown,
Falls dying from his tottering throne !
But one is there whose soul-lit eyes
Bear the deep blue of country skies,
A poet, who in all things sees
New meanings and new mysteries;
And near the tree amid the throng,
Outwells from him this artless song:

I

Enshrined amid the ancient wood,
Long ages gone our beech-tree stood,
Unchallenged king of solitude !

II

In slumberous summers long ago
It felt the woodland breezes blow
And toss its branches to and fro.

III

It braved a hundred winter's harms,
It mocked the tempest's wild alarms,
And took the whirlwind in its arms;

IV
And beat by storms of snow and rain,
A conscious Titan, in disdain
Defied the pigmy hurricane.

V

Men spared it for a stranger's name,
Who moulders now unknown to fame —
Dust in the dust from whence he came !

VI

And years pass on, and ages roll,

And no man knows where roams the soul
That moved the hand to trace that scroll.

VII
And no one knows, on land or deep,
Where nature holds him in her keep, —
The still place where he fell asleep.

VIII

And no one knows what voids of night,
What starry domes of trembling light
His soul has met upon its flight.

IX

And Fame no proud word of him saith,
He only left his name — a breath
Blown from the shoreless seas of death.

X

And years pass on, and ages roll;
And no man knows where roams the soul
That moved the hand to trace that scroll!

THE EASTER MAIDEN'S HYMN OF PRAISE.

I FEEL a solemn sanctity, Sweet rest of soul is mine,
My heart abides in pious peace, —
(My bonnet sets divine !)
Grace, like a river, fills my soul,
In chastened joy I sit,

I feel religion's deepest power, —
(My sacque's a perfect fit.)
A holy fervor penetrates
My soul's remotest nooks,
An earnest, chastened, fervid joy, —
(How neat that ribbon looks !)
The good man tells of Christian peace,
The organ's anthem swells,
I bathe in streams of pure delight —
(My dress cost more than Nell's !)

O holy rest! O, Sabbath calm !
O chastened peace serene !
I feel thy deep, abiding spell !
(How dowdy is Miss Green !)
I feel a pure, religious glow,
O rapture undefined!
(I know my bonnet looks so nice
To those who sit behind !)

JOHN BILLINGTON'S JOURNEY.

JOHN BILLINGTON, on April first, went forth from New Orleans,
Dressed in a clean white linen suit, a well-groomed man of means.
He wore a pair of russet shoes, a spotless white cravat,
A pair of thin silk stockings, and an excellent straw hat.

He travelled up to Birmingham; the mercury went down,
And so he bought a woollen coat of good substantial brown.
" I hate superfluous truck," says he, " to lug from day to day,
And so I'll put the thick coat on and throw the thin away."

Then on to Chattanooga flew the limited express;

He felt his pantaloons were thin, and shivered in distress;
He bought a thick black woollen pair, and still pursued his quest,
And journeyed on to Richmond, where he bought another vest.

When he reached Philadelphia it rained a pouring flood,
And hence he found his russet shoes were poor things for the mud;
He bought a stout dark-leather pair to wade the watery float,
And journeyed onward to New York and bought an overcoat.

Next day he went to Boston; the shivers made him creep,
The air was cold as Greenland and the snow was four feet deep;
But bravely did he sally forth, with chill and cold half dead,
His overcoat all buttoned up, a straw hat on his head.

A straw hat and an overcoat, a snow-storm and all that,
The youngsters of that classic town all shouting " Shoot that hat!
" The strange concatenation made the cultured people smile,
And young musicians whistled shrill, " Where did you get that tile?"

He rushed and bought a sealskin cap, stopped at the " Hub " a day,
And then resumed his journey on his southern homeward way;
He came to New York city, found it very sultry there,
And threw away his overcoat, it was too warm to wear.

He went to Philadelphia and dropped his sealskin cap,
He portioned his apparel round to each place on the map,
His coat and vest were scattered on successive sultry noons,
He hung the lines of longitude with cast-off pantaloons.

John Billington, on April twelfth, came back to New Orleans,
Dressed in a clean, white linen suit, a well-groomed man of means;
He wore a pair of russet shoes, a spotless white cravat,
A pair of thin silk stockings, and an excellent straw hat.

SPRING POTERY.

I SKIN out behin' the barn, the first warm day in spring,
And go to rattlin' potery out, a-ting-a-ling-a-ling.
It busts, jest like volcaners bust, an' comes a-rollin' out,
I never try to hol' it in, but alius let her spout!
An' I like potery better'n pie, or any kin' er sass,
An hanker for't like winter cows a-hankerin' for grass;
It bubbles up like yeast in spring in bread thet's partly riz,
An' aggervates yer sistem like a case er roomatiz.

The angels pack their winter clo'es— their clo'es from head to feet —
An' douse perfum'ry on 'em — at's w'at makes the air so sweet —
The flirtin' heavens, they sass the hills 4th win's an' peltin' showers,
An' then the jolly, gigglin' hills, they sass right back 4th flowers.

The earth, whose jints hez been so stiff 4th frosty roomatiz,
Jest sticks her sunshine plaster on, an' goes about her biz,
An' Natur', she jest swallers down her tonic uv warm win',
Shakes off the blues, an' then resolves to try the thing agin.

The brook thet's been a-grumblin' on way un'erneath the snow,
Breaks into sich a laffin' song it makes the mayflowers grow.
Look here ! W'y shouldn't I blossom out, an' cast off winter's gloom ?
W'y shouldn't I bust in potery ez mayflowers bust in bloom ?

The brooks go peddlin' potery; the robins strew it roun',
The bobolink jest slings it, an' makes the air resoun.
In flowin' lines er crocuses, no man should dare to skip,
God writes his purtiest potery on his medder manuscrip'.

THIS is an age of lightning,

The world hums on its way,
And lightning lights its lamp by night,
And pulls its load by day;
And he who seeks its prizes,
The world's applause or gains,
Must stir the lightning in his blood,
And mix it in his brains.
Right on it spins, a whirling whizz
With fierce electric gleams,
Right down " the ringing grooves of change "
The blazing courser streams;
Then watch your chance and jump aboard,
Throw off your heavy chains,
And stir the lightning in your blood,
And mix it in your brains.

THE FANCY-WORK MAIDEN.

TT N' so you kinder wanter know w'y I broke off with
It warn't because she warn't a good an' mighty purty gal:
For there ain't a blessed star in heaven shines brighter than her eyes,
An' her cheeks are jest like peaches on the trees er Paradise !

An' her smile is like the sunshine spilt upon a flower bed,
An' her hair like sproutin' sunbeams on the garding of her head,
An' her laff is like a singin' brook that bubbles as it passes
Thro' the stuck-up tiger lilies, an' the purty smellin' grasses.

An' I told her that I loved her, much as forty times a day,
But she hadn't much time to bother, an' kep' on with her crowshay;
Wen I plumped right down afore her, plumb upon my very knees, She said,
" Git off my ric-rac, an' you're rumplin' up my frieze."

An' I tried to talk of love, an things, an' told her would die
Unless she smiled upon my soot. She simply said,
" Oh, my ! You've tore my purty tidy down, an' —- hain't ye got no eyes? —
You've planted them big feet o' yourn on them air tapestries! "

An' she wove in big flamingoes, snipes, an' turkeys on her rugs,
An' she painted yaller poodles on her mother's 'lasses jugs,
An' she painted purple angels on majenta colored plaques,
An' five orange-colored cherubs, with blue wings behin' their backs.
An' w'en I talked of love an' stuff, she'd talk of rugs an' lace,
An' ax me would I take my feet from off thet Chiny vase.
I'd say, " My heart's love, O, be mine ! be mine ! be wholly mine !"
She'd say, " You've got your elbows mixed in that silk skein er twine."

Now I'm goin to Arizony for to do a cowboy's work,
Driven forth from civil'zation by the cuss er fancy-work,
But her smile will alius hant me, alius in my visions play,
Framed in latest styles of ric-rac, with a backgroun' of crowshay.

"I would make Boston a suburb of glory." — SAM JONES.

 M AKE Boston a suburb of glory,
Sam Jones?
Do you know what such sacrilege means ?
I fear you have not read the story,
Sam Jones,
Of that city of culture and beans.
You are sailing through breakers and rocks,
Sam Jones,
A dangerous sea you are tossed on;
Hereafter be sure in your talks,
Sam Jones,
To make glory a suburb of Boston !

THE INVENTOR.

HE had a startling genius, but somehow it didn't emerge ;
Always on the evolution of things that wouldn't evolve;
Always verging toward some climax, but he never reached the verge;
Always nearing the solution of some theme he could not solve.

And he found perpetual motion, but a cog wheel set awry
Burst his complex apparatus and he could not get it fixed;
And he made a life elixir — if you drank you'd never die —
But the druggist spoilt the compound when the medicine was mixed.

And he made a flying vessel that would navigate the air,
A gorgeous steamer of the heavens, a grand aerial boat,
A matchless paragon of skill, a thing beyond compare,
And the only trouble with it — he could never make it float.

And he found a potent acid that would change red dirt to gold;
But the tube from which he poured it had some trouble with its squirt,
The gold held in solution and would not let go its hold,
A,nd the dirt, in dogged stubbornness, it still continued dirt.

And he made a great catholicon to cure all disease,
A general panacea for every ache and pain,
But first he tried it on himself, his stomach ache to ease,
And it killed him very quickly — and he did not try again.

THE AUCTIONEER'S GIFT.

THE auctioneer leaped on a chair, and bold and loud and clear,
He poured his cataract of words — just like an auctioneer.

An auction sale of furniture, where some hard mortgagee
Was bound to get his money back, and pay his lawyer's fee.

A humorist of wide renown, this doughty auctioneer,
His horse-play raised the loud guffaw, and brought the answering jeer;
He scattered round his jokes, like rain, on the unjust and the just:
Sam Sleeman said he "laffed so much he thought that he would bust."

He knocked down bureaus, beds, and stoves, and clocks and chandeliers,
And a grand piano, which he swore would " last a thousand years ";
He rattled out the crockery, and sold the silverware, —
At last they passed him up, to sell, a little baby's chair.

"How much? how much? come, make a bid; is all your money spent?"
And then a cheap, facetious wag came up and bid, "One cent."
Just then a sad-faced woman, who stood in silence there,
Broke down and cried, " My baby's chair! My poor, dead baby's chair!"

" Here, -madam, take your baby's chair," said the softened auctioneer,
"I know it's value all too well — my baby died last year—
And if the owner of the chair, our friend, the mortgagee,
Objects to this proceeding, let him send the bill to me ! "

Gone was the tone of raillery; the humorist auctioneer
Turned shamefaced from his audience to brush away a tear;
The laughing crowd was awed and still, no tearless eye was there
When the weeping woman reached and took her little baby's chair.

THE AGRICULTUREAL EDITOR'S POEM.

I WOULD flee from the city's rule and law,
From its fashion and form cut loose,
And go where the strawberry grows on its straw,

And the gooseberry grows on its goose;
Where the catnip tree is climbed by the cat,
As she crouches for her prey —
The guileless and unsuspecting rat,
On the rattan bush at play.

I will watch at ease the saffron cow
And the cowlet in their glee,
As they leap in joy from bough to bough,
On the top of the cowslip tree;
Where the musical partridge drums on his drum,
And the woodchuck chucks his wood,
And the dog devours the dogwood plum
In the primitive solitude.

Oh, let me drink from the moss-grown pump
That was hewn from the pumpkin tree,
Eat mush and milk from a rural stump
(From form and fashion free) —
New gathered mush from the mushroom vine,
And milk from the milkweed sweet,
With luscious pineapple from the pine —
Such food as the gods might eat!

And then to the whitewashed dairy I'll turn,
Where the dairymaid hastening hies,
Her ruddy and golden red butter to churn
From the milk of her butterflies;
And I'll rise at morn with the early bird,
To the fragrant farmyard pass,
When the farmer turns his beautiful herd
Of grasshoppers out to grass.

THE QUESTION.

THE orator gets up to speak
And starts out with an opening shriek,
" The question naturally arises.
" Well, orator, as I surmise,
These questions frequently arise
And stand up waiting for replies. —
The question naturally arises.

It comes in hours of grief or mirth,
At the gates of death, or the gates of birth;
The question naturally arises, —
The question, " Wherefore ? Whither ? Why ? "
The unanswering earth, the silent sky,
Stand dumb, vouchsafing no reply. —
The question naturally arises.

Fate crooks its questioning finger joint —
A huge interrogation point, —
The question naturally arises;
It motions on the curious child,
The maid, with trusting heart and mild,
The youth, with passions hot and wild; —
The question naturally arises.

It comes to greatest and to least,
A guest unbidden at the feast. —
The question naturally arises.
" What means it all? " the spectre saith, "
This fitful, momentary breath,
Choked in the icy grip of death ? " —

The question naturally arises.

We hear it on that awful shore,
It mingles with its sullen roar; —
The question naturally arises.
" What lies," it asks, " beyond the mist,
Those troubled waters, twilight-kissed,
The sunset clouds of amethyst? "
The question naturally arises.

THE DIPPER AND THE SEA.

HE held a dipper in his hand,
And bravely did he ply,
 With all the strength at his command,
To dip the ocean dry.
" And all the ships that sail," says he,
" And go from land to land,
On the dry bottom of the sea
Shall sink into the sand.

" The waves are powerless to resist;
Through me fulfilled shall be
The words of the evangelist,
' There shall be no more sea.'
" And so he plies his dipper fast,
And does not cease to try,
As long as strength and life shall last,
To dip the ocean dry.

And like this madman, even we,
With little dippers try
To drain the vastness of the sea,

And dip the ocean dry.
The sea of knowledge with its din
Before us breaks, and we, —
We thrust our little dippers in,
And think we've drained the sea.

And bound within a narrow creed,
Shut in by walls and towers,
We deem we have no further need, —
The truth of God is ours.
Then let the endless babblers be,
Who for more wisdom cry,
We've thrust our dippers in the sea,
And drained the ocean dry.

THE WAY TO SLEEPTOWN.

THE town of Sleeptown is not far,
Timbuctoo or China,
For it's right near by in Blinkton County,
In the State of Drowsylina;
It's just beyond the Thingumbob hills,
Not far from Nodville Centre,
But you must be drawn thro' the Valley of Yawn,
Or the town you cannot enter.
And this is the way,
They say, they say.
That Baby goes to Sleeptown!

He starts from the City of Odearme,
Thro' Boohoo street he totters,
Until he comes to Dontcry Corners
By the shore of the Sleeping Waters,

Then he comes to Johnny-Jump-Up hills,
And the nodding
Toddlebom mountains,
And straight does he go thro' the Vale of Heigho,
And drink from the Drowsy Fountains.
And this is the way,
They say, they say,
That Baby goes to Sleeptown !

By Twilight Path thro' the Nightcap Hills
The little feet must toddle,
Thro' the dewy gloom of Flyaway Forest,
By the drowsy peaks of Noddle;
And never a sound doth Baby hear,
For not a leaf doth quiver,
From the Little Dream Gap in the Hills of Nap
To the Snoozequehanna River.
And this is the way,
They say, they say,
That Baby goes to Sleeptown !

Away he flies over Bylow Bridge,
Through Lullaby Lane to wander,
And on thro' the groves of Moonshine Valley
By the hills of Wayoffyonder;
And then does the fairies' flying horse
The sleepy Baby take up —
Until they enter at Jumpoff Centre
The Peekaboo Vale of Wakeup.
And this is the way,
They say, they say,
That Baby comes from Sleeptown!

MY ANARCHIST BORDER.

WOULD I consort with Anarchists,
And mix and drink and dine ?
Oh, yes, I board an Anarchist —
He is a chum of mine.
A ruthless enemy to law,
This boarder that I mention,
A friend to lawless unconstraint,
A foe to all convention.

And though I diligently try
To keep my home in trim,
I harbor this wild Anarchist
And grow attached to him.
His incoherent creed by day
He blusters and he babbles;
By night he howls it in our ears,
Or garrulously gabbles.

The right of private ownership
He strenuously denies,
He rends and tears my property
Before my very eyes;
And in his fierce and lawless moods
He'll beat us and belay us;
Oh, he's confusion's champion,
A hierarch of chaos !

There are no rights that he respects,
No sanctity reveres;
Regards not customs, creeds, nor texts,

Experience nor years.
No laws or constitutions bind
This Anarchist of ours,
Nor popes, nor principalities,
Nor potencies, nor powers.

He is a hopeless radical,
A sworn iconoclast —
No plan or purpose for to-day,
No reverence for the past.
You ask me why I keep him, then?
Well, I can answer, maybe,
Because — because he calls me " Dad,"
And I — I call him " Baby."

THE SONG THAT SILAS SUNG.

NEIGHBOR SILAS sting a song
Every day his whole life long,
Sung it gladly 'neath the cloud
That hung o'er him like a shroud;
Or when sunbeams with their play
Gleamed and glorified his way,
Like a shower of joy outflung
Was the song that Silas sung:
Let the howlers howl,
And the scowlers scowl,
And the growlers growl,
And the gruff gang go it;
But behind the night
There's a plenty of light,
And everythings all right,
And I know it !

Like the battle drum to me
Was that song of victory,
Like the flute's exultant strain
'Mid the wounded and the slain,
Like the quick blood-stirring fife
On the battle-plain of life;
Far and free the echoes rung
Of the song that Silas sung:
Let the howlers howl,
And the scowlers scowl,
And the growlers growl,
And the gruff gang go it;
But behind the night
There's a plenty of light,
And everythings all rights
And I know it!

Silas' soul has taken flight,
Passed in music through the night,
Through the shadow chill and gray
And gone singing on its way;
But the quaint song that was his
Cheers the saddened silences;
Still glad triumph notes are flung
From the song that Silas sung:
Let the howlers howl,
And the scowlers scowl,
And the growlers growl,
And the gruff gang go it;
But behind the night
There's a plenty of light,

And everythings all right,
And I know it !

THE POET AT PLAY.

I SAW a poet in the crowd,
His voice was gay, his laugh was loud;
Perplexed I questioned : " Is this he,
The laurelled Priest of Minstrelsy?"

For his sweet rhythmic words had stole
In a strange music to my soul,
As if from midnight deeps had rung
The accents of a seraph tongue.

I pictured him by woodland streams,
A silent mystic, wrapped in dreams,
Who talked with mountains as with men,
And with the voices of the glen.

I deemed that all his thoughts were high
As any star within the sky;
As calm as evening when caressed
By twilight breezes from the west.

For far abroad his songs had flown,
Like singing birds, to every zone,
And weary souls in toiling throngs
Had learned to love him for his songs.

And they who sank 'neath fortune's frowns,
Whose brows were crowned with iron crowns,
Felt through the midnight of their wrongs

The noonday sunlight of his songs.

But now, mid laughter, mirth, and play
He sang a village roundelay,
Forgetful of his lettered fame,
Forgetful of his world-loved name.

He led the children in their sports,
Their joy was more than praise of courts,
And the glad laughter in their eyes,
Than fickle fame's delusive prize.

And then I thought, " 'Tis better so,
For he who sings should surely know
The heart he sings to, and the soul
Be spread before him like a scroll."

THEY DON'T MAKE CONNECTIONS.

W'EN I was a little kid,
Not more than three feet high,
I used to try to find the place
The earth hitched on the sky. Yes,
I'd go prancin' roun' to find,
In frisky, childish mirth,
The big suspender button by which
The sky held up the earth.
But tho' I waltzed aroun' like sin,
An' searched in all directions,
I alius foun' the earth an' sky
Didn't seem to make connections.

Now w'en I see a man purtends

To be all-fired good,
An' most too pure an' jest to live
In our poor neighborhood;
W'en he parades his virtues roun'
For everyone to note,
Till we expect to see his wings
Sprout through his overcoat; —
I say, " Ole Slyboots, you're a fraud,
In spite of your perfections;
I've alius foun' the earth an' sky
Don't seem to make connections."

W'en I fight my besettin' sins
I have a tarnal rub,
Jest like Archangel Michael
W'en he fit with Beelzebub.
So w'en a man sez he is good
As any ancient saint,
W'y ! all the more he sez he is
The more I say he ain't!
For you can box the compass roun',
An' go in all directions,
You'll alius find the earth an' sky
Don't seem to make connections.

Now, there's my wife, Matildy Jane,
She hain't no monstrous sins,
She's alius tried to treat us fair, —
Me, Peter an' the twins;
But get her on the rampage once
She makes consid'ble dust,
We alius think w'en she explodes
The crack o' doom has bust!

An' so, I say, go where you will,
An' search in all directions,
You'll alius find the earth an' sky
Don't seem to make connections.

A FATAL DISEASE.

HE was a man of giant length
And strength;
 With limbs strong as an iron rod,
And health of an immortal god,
With courage that defied all troubles,
And spirits sparkling o'er like bubbles —
If ever was a healthy man, Twas Dan.

But full is fickle fortune's smile
Of guile;
For Dan brought home one day, alack!
A patent medicine almanac,
All full of long and learned theses
Upon the symptoms of diseases;
Dan read the symptoms great and small
And had them all!
Said he, the while his breath came quick,
" I'm sick.
For if these symptoms tell me true,
I've surely got tic-douloureux,
The gastric fever and bronchitis
And cerebro-spinal-meningitis.
Go fetch a lawyer with a quill
To make my will!

" I've got congestion of the brain,

'Tis plain.
No balm a man like me can ease,
In the last stage of Bright's disease;
True symptoms — and all faith I grant 'em —
Proclaim the cholera infantum.
And, tell me, is that lawyer here ? Oh, dear! "

The lawyer came, wrote with his quill,
The will;
The patient then turned on his side
And in intensest torment died.
They wrote upon his mausoleum,
These words —and any man can see 'em, —
" A guileless youth, who died, alack !
Of Almanack! "

THE MAN WHO MISS THE TRAIN.

I LOAF aroun' the depo' jest to see the Pullman scoot,
An' to see the people scamper w'en they hear the engine toot;
But w'at makes the most impression on my som'w'at active
brain,
Is the careless men who get there jest in time to miss the train.

An' some cuss the railroad comp'ny, an' some loudly cuss their stars,
An' some jest gallop down the track an' try to catch the cars;
An' some with a loud laff an' joke will poultice up their pain, —
Var'us kin's er people get there jest in time to miss the train.

An' there is many deepos an' flag-stations 'ithout name,
Along the Grand Trunk Railroad thet leads to wealth an' fame,
An' men rush to these deepos, as fast as they can fly,
As the Train of Oppertunity jest goes a-thunderin by.

They rush down to the stations with their hair all stood on end,
As the platform of the tail-end car goes whirlin roun' the bend;
An' some men groan an' cry aloud, an' some conceal their pain,
Wen they find thet they have got there jest in time to miss the train.

But the cars puff through the valleys, an' go a-whirlin by,
An' float their banners of w'ite smoke, like flags of victory;
They leap the flowin' rivers, an' through the tunnels grope,
An' cross the Mountains of Despair to the Tableland of Hope.

The Grand Trunk Railroad of Success, it runs through every clime,
But the Cars of Oppertunity they go on schedule time,
An' never are their brakes reversed — they won't back up . again
To take the men who get there jest in time to miss the train.

SONGS OF THE CORN.

I HEARD the corn at noonday,
And all its rustling leaves
Told summer tales, like swallows
That build beneath the eaves.

As if it drank the sunshine
And gave it forth in strong,
Unfaltering, leafy accents
Of multitudinous song, —

It sang a song of victory,
Of triumph over fears;
And waved its silken banners
And clashed its leafy spears.

I heard the corn at midnight;
In tones of sad dismay,
It sang like those who sing to-day
The songs of yesterday.

I heard the shadowy sobbings
Of unreturning hosts,
The march of phantom soldiery,
The tread of viewless ghosts.

And I walked with reverent footsteps
Through the maize field in the morn,
I knew the spirits of pain had wept
All night among the corn,

THE BROOK BENEATH THE SNOW.

WAY down in dad's ol' medder, where the pussy willers
I used to go an' listen to the brook beneath the snow;
Above I heerd the roarin' win' an' saw the snow-gust whirl;
But the brook beneath the snow an' ice danced singin' like a girl.

I'd put my ear down to the ice, I didn' min' the col', An' w'en
I heerd its music there wuz summer in my soul!
An' we'n dad licked me, an' my heart 'ud bile an' overflow,
I would go an' hear the music of the brook beneath the snow.

An' then my sobs 'ud change to shouts, an' sorrer change to glee,
For it strewed along its music from the mountain to the sea;
An' I'd stretch my ear to hear it, an' my heart 'ud swell an' glow,
W'en I listened to the music of the brook beneath the snow.

Since then the wintry blasts of life have blown me here an' there,

An' snowstorms they have blocked my way an' hedged me everywhere;
But sheltered from the harrycane, within the valley low,
I listen for the music of the brook beneath the snow.

For I know beneath the snow an' ice that there is golden sand,
By that glorious streak uv melody that wiggles through the land;
The storm beats hard; the wind is high; I cannot hear it blow,
For I listen to the music of the brook beneath the snow.

AT the debatin' club las' night we all discussed a cure "
"Fer the debilitated state of English lit'rachure,"
"The stuff thet's writ fer folks," I said, "don't move 'em an' delight 'em,
Because the folks who write the things don't know enough to write em."

" The folks who write, they stuff their heads in some big cyclopedy,
W'ich ain't no place fer mental food to feed the poor an' needy,
They're huntin' on an em'ty shelf, like poor ol' Mother . Hubbard,
And go right by the open door of Mother Natur's cupboard.

They crawl into some libery, fer from the worl's inspection,
Bury themselves in books be-end all hope of resurrection;
They cry out from their tombs, in w'ich no sun nor star can glisten,
An' weep because the livin' worl' don't fin' no time to listen."

Then Elder Pettengill he asked, " Can you sejest a cure
Fer the debilitated state of English lit'rachure ? "
" Ain't none: our authors' ignorance is far too dark for lightin',
While we who know enough to write hain't got no time for writin'."

THE OLD MAN SINGS.

THERE'S a wobble in the jingle and a stumble in the metre,
And the accent might be clearer and the volume be completer,

And there might be much improvement in the stress and intonation,
And a polish might be added to the crude pronunciation;
But there's music, like the harper's played before the ancient kings,
When the old man takes the fiddle and goes feeling for the strings,
There is laughter choked with teardrops when the old man sings.

And we form a ring about him and we place him in the middle,
And he hugs up to his withered cheek the poor old broken fiddle,
And a smile comes on his features as he hears the strings' vibration,
And he sings the songs of long ago with faltering intonation;
And phantoms from the distant past his broken music brings,
And trooping from their dusty graves come long-forgotten things,
When he tunes the ancient fiddle and the old man sings.

We let the broken man play on upon the broken fiddle,
And we press around to hear him, as he sits there in the middle;
The sound of many wedding bells in all the music surges, —
Then we hear their clamor smothered by the sound of funeral dirges.
'Tis the story of his lifetime that in the music rings —
And every life's a blind man's tune that's played on broken strings —
And so we sit in silence while the old man sings.

THE TURNPIKE RODE.

W 'EN I want to go to Boston, some thirty miles away,
I hitch the mareat 4 A. M., an' start at peep o' day ;
Thro' cross-road lanes she pulls along as if she felt
her load,
An' don't get down to business till she strikes the turnpike
road.

But w'en she strikes the turnpike road, to trot is on'y play,
An' she sniffs a smell of Boston w'en it's fifteen miles away,

She fergits her heaves an' spavins an' don't seem to min' her load,
But jest cracks thro' the atmosphere along the turnpike road.

An' the rat-tat of her hoof-beats is like the rum-tum-tum
W'en armies march to victory behin' the battle drum;
W'en she pints her nose to Boston, she needs no spur nor
goad, But whirls the worl' beneath her feet along the turnpike
road.
An' men are jest like my ol' mare, along the cross-road lanes,
They have no ginger in their blood, no lightnin' in their
brains: An' they get apt to kick an' balk, an' groan beneath their
load, An' loaf an' cuss their stars, unless they strike the turnpike road.

But don't get discouraged, fellers, don't kick, an' sheer an' shirk;
The turnpike road is jest be-end the big swamps of Hard Work.
In Lazy Lane an' Whiskey Alley don't linger with yer load,
They'll land you in the bogs at last, far from the turnpike road.

An' don't try Mortgage Avenue, thet lands in swamps of
Debt. W'en you see their flamin' guideboards, jest keep your peepers shet;
An' don't loaf on Pleasure Common, but buckle to your load,
An' jest keep peggin' thro' the dust, an' strike the turnpike road.

Don't linger at the cross-roads, an' loaf roun' in the lanes,
The worl's highways are open to men of pluck an' brains;
Trot on an' git yer second wind, don't mind yer heavy load,
An' dash out with a spanking pace upon the turnpike road.

WHERE THE SUN GOES DOWN.

THE road that passed his father's door
He thought stretched on forevermore;
Through fragrant vales of tangled grass,

O'er many a misty mountain pass,
Out into wonders unexpressed
Beyond the cloudlands of the West,
Through lands and cities of renown,
To where the mighty sun goes down.

And so he left his father's door
And said, " I will return no more."

He travelled forth beyond the bridge,
He climbed the lofty mountain ridge,
He passed the river and the town
To find out where the sun went down;
But when he sank at close of day,
The sunset still was far away.

He trod through many a wind-swept glen;
In mighty towns he mixed with men;
The breath of many an alien breeze
Tossed him o'er unfamiliar seas;
He breathed the spicy gale that blows
From Southern archipelagoes.
And in the quiet Eastern calm
He sought sweet sleep beneath the palm,
But when he looked at close of day,
The sunset still was far away.

He thought to leave his father's door
And travel on forevermore.

A withered pilgrim, bent and gray,
Kept on his unfamiliar way.
Deep versed in lands, a man of men,

A universal citizen,
He circled all the earth : once more
He stood before his father's door —
Though many years his father slept
Upon the mountain-side, unwept —
He stood there wrinkled, worn, and brown,
He stood there as the sun went down,
And in the twilight dim and gray
The sunset was not far away.

Out from the many millions hurled
He sank down, weary of the world,
With all his tired journey o'er,
To die beside his father's door,
And said, a sad smile on his brow,
" I pass beyond the sunset now."

" HULLO! "

W 'EN you see a man in woe,
Walk right up and say "hullo !"
Say "hullo," an' "how d'ye do !" "
How's the world a usin' you?"
Slap the fellow on his back,
Bring your han' down with a whack;
Waltz right up, an' don't go slow,
Grin an' shake an' say " hullo ! "

Is he clothed in rags ? O sho !
Walk right up an' say " hullo ! "
Rags is but a cotton roll
Jest for wrappin' up a soul;
An' a soul is worth a true

Hale an' hearty " how d'ye do ! "
Don't wait for the crowd to go,
Walk right up and say " hullo ! "

W'en big vessels meet, they say,
They saloot an' sail away.
Jest the same are you an' me,
Lonesome ships upon a sea;
Each one sailing his own jog
For a port beyond the fog.
Let your speakin' trumpet blow,
Lift your horn an' cry "hullo ! "

Say "hullo," an' "how d'ye do ! "
Other folks are good as you.
Wen you leave your house of clay,
Wanderin' in the Far-Away,
Wen you travel through the strange
Country t'other side the range,
The' the souls you've cheered will know
Wh6 you be, an' say " hullo ! "

THE KINDS OF MAN.

SOW yer garding on a hillside thet's slantin' to the south
Ye'll raise such luscious garding sass, 'twill melt right il yer mouth;
An' cabbidges an' cowcumbers an' ev'ry kine er plant
Jest hump theirselves an' grow like grass upon a souther slant.

But take the tough ol' red oak tree, an' it will droop an' blight,
Unless it has the col' north wind to wrastle with an' fight;
It stumps the rough northeaster, defies the wind and rain,
An' grips the bottom of the hills, an' fights the harricane.

Some men are jest like garding sass, jest like the cabbidge plant,
They on'y grow upon the hills thet hev a southward slant;
They grow, like pigweeds in July, an' on'y live for fun,
An' hol' their mouths up toward the south, an' jest fill up 'ith sun.

An' some are like the tough red oak, all seamed 'ith many a scar,
By fightin' storms thet smite the hills beneath the northern star;
The whirlwinds seem to make 'em strong, the cyclones make em' grow;
They grow to giants w'ile they fight the lightnin' an' the snow.

COLUMBUS.

COLUMBUS was, they tell us now,
A man of flaw and fleck, —
A man who steered a pirate prow,
And trod a slaver's deck.
In narrow bigot blindness curled,
Cruel and vain was he —
To such was given to lift a world
From out the darkened sea.

Though weak and cruel, vain, untrue,
From all earth's high and low
.God picked this man, His work to do,,
Four hundred years ago.
There in the distance standeth he,
Bound on his mighty quest,
This rough old Admiral of the Sea,
Still pointing toward the West.

There stands he on his westward prow,
A man entirely strong;

So great, the bald truth spoken now
Can never do him wrong.
Though slaver, pirate, he might be,
He had that gift of fate, —
That wise and sane insanity
That makes the great man great.

FATHER'S JOURNEY.

HE GOES.

WHEN father goes to Gunjiwump
He keeps the family on a jump.
Jim hauls the wagon in the yard
To grease the axles up with lard;
He rubs the old horse down with care,
And gets the whip in good repair;
He mends the harness up with string
And makes it strong as anything;
He cleans the wheels up at the pump,
When father goes to Gunjiwump.
He scrapes and scours for hours and hours,
And flits and flutters on the jump,
For we all have to worry and hurry and skurry
When father goes to Gunjiwump.

When father goes to Gunjiwump
He doesn't go like any gump;
He has his boots greased up in style
With the best kind of linseed "ile."
This is the task for little Joe,
Of lamentation and of woe;
He bears on hard and rubs it in

With mutterings, which to speak were sin;
He gives the cowhides many a thump,
And hates the name of Gunjiwump.

For it just doubles our toils and troubles,
And masses them a solid lump;
'Tis an aggregation of tribulation
When father goes to Gunjiwump.

When father goes to Gunjiwump
They gather round him in a clump,
Matilda, Martha, Jane and Sue,
Each with some special task to do.
Matilda tries to part his hair,
Marth gets his whiskers in repair,
Jane fixes his suspenders right,
And Sue she gets his collar tight;
They fuss and fuddle on the jump
When father goes to Gunjiwump.
They fix his tackle, and coax and cackle,
And gather round him in a clump;
They fasten and button whatever he's got on
When father goes to Gunjiwump.

We all sink down, a helpless lump,
When father's gone to Gunjiwump;
We only lie around and shirk,
For we are all too tired to work.
But mother says, " He looked as nice
As if he had been kept on ice;
Not many young swells look so trim
And dickydandyfied as him;
To beat his get-up, I will stump

Most any dude in Gunjiwump."
Though bruised and battered, we are all flattered,
A self-congratulating clump;
In glowing phrases we sound his praises
When father's gone to Gunjiwump.

HE COMES.

When father comes from Gunjiwump
He keeps the family on a jump.
Like Caesar on his triumph car,
Young Tom espies him from afar,
And jubilantly runs from home
To bid him welcome into Rome.
He spies him by the alder clump,
The conqueror from Gunjiwump.
With his trophies of candy he makes himself handy,
And on the new drum does he joyously thump.
Like an army with banners, a host with hosannas,
Does father come from Gunjiwump.

When father comes from Gunjiwump
We run to meet him by the pump,—
Matilda, Martha, Jane and Sue,
Each with her special hullabaloo;
And quickly scoots out from the shed
The swift and spinning form of Ned.
It seems like Gabriel with his trump
When father comes from Gunjiwump.
We fuss and flutter, and spurt and sputter, —
All dull, domestic duties dump;
'lis a jubilation, a glad vacation
When father comes from Gunjiwump,

When father comes from Gunjiwump
We gather round him in a clump;
Matilda gets a gingham dress
To aggravate her loveliness,
Marth gets her shoes; a colored skein
Of cotton yarn for sister Jane.
For Sue and ma his pockets dump
A mighty pack from Gunjiwump.
And we spread each trophy upon the " sofy,"

A self-congratulating clump,
And talk and clatter, and shout and chatter,
When father comes from Gunjiwump.
When father comes from Gunjiwump,
He throws his clothing in a clump,
His jacket on the cellar door,
His boots and collar on the floor.
His vesture, in sad disarray,
We put to rights some time next day.
Tom says it makes the family "hump "
When father comes from Gunjiwump.
But we're glad of the worry, the hurry and skurry,
That keeps us on the constant jump,
Each thinks of the trophy that lies on the "sofy"
When father comes from Gunjiwump.

NO FOREIGNERS NEED APPLY.

THE Anti-Immigration club met at McDougall's store,
And swore to keep all foreigners from fair Columbia's shore.
There was Pat McCoy, Hans Schwatzenmeyer, Won Lung,Monsieur Le Bounce,
And an exiled Russian Nihilist whose name you couldn't pronounce.

" We'll keep them bloody furriners, begorra, where they be,
Atother side the wather, sors," said Michael Pat McGee;
" Dhose Dootchmans mans moost shtay avay und keep dis coundtry oudt,
Nor coom," said Hans, "to shteal mine beer, or eat mine
sauerkraut."

" Oui, messieurs," said Monsieur Le Bounce, " dees countree ees la belle,
La grande, la grosse, la magnifique, ve love it well, ver' well!
Ve keep de Frenchmen from its shore and leev in quiet ease,
And then, like true-born Yankees, ve vill eat our frogs in peace!"

"The blarsted Britisher must go," said John Bull Jinks, " must go;
Faw — aw — we have no room, no space few aliens, doncher- know."
"John Chinaman we'll dlive away," said Sam Wing Lee, " and then,
We Melican folks will have no men but just us Melican men."

STAN' UP AN' GET HIT.

THIS life is a fight that has got to be fit.
The best thing you can do is stan' up an' get hit, —
Stan' up, like John L., through the bruises an' pain,
An' not dodge and skedaddle an' skulk, like Kilrain;
Jest square off with fate for the set-to of life,
An' keep your fists clinched for the tug of the strife.
Jest tighten your belt, pull the buckle a bit,
Stagger back from the blow, an' stan' up an' get hit!

Luck loves the hard hitter and glorifies grit,
An' smiles on the man who Stan's up an' gets hit;
Tho' fate strikes out strong, with a blow 'twixt the eyes,
It loves the stout soul who still fights and defies.
The fight is not gained by the strong or the fleet,

But by the grim chap who don't know he is beat.
This life is a fight that has got to be fit.
The best thing you can do is stan' up an' get hit.

Wen you see the blow coming don't falter and flit, —
Jest strike back yerself an' stan' up an' get hit.
Though fate is a fighter that never will fly,
Don't throw up the sponge till yer ready to die;
Tho' at times yer eyes swim, yer head whirls like a top
Till yer ready ter die, don't get ready ter drop,
But feel thro' the darkness, an' brace up a bit—
Jest pray for more strenk, an' stan' up an' get hit !

FAMILY FINANCIERING.

THEY tell me you work for a dollar a day, —
How is it you clothe your six boys on such pay?"
" I know you will think it conceited and queer,
But I do it because I'm a good financier.

"There's Pete, John, Joe, Jim, William, and Ned,
A half dozen boys to be clothed and be fed.

" I buy for them all good, plain victuals to eat,
But clothing—I only buy clothing for Pete.

" When Pete's clothes are too small for him to get on,
My wife makes 'em over and gives 'em to John.

"When for John, who is ten, they have grown out of date,
She just makes 'em over for Jim, who is eight.

" When for Jim they've become too ragged to fix,

She just makes 'em over for Joe, who is six.

" And when little Joseph can wear 'em no more,
She just makes 'em over for Bill, who is four.

" And when for young Bill they no longer will do,
She just makes 'em over for Ned, who is two.

" So you see if I get enough clothing for Pete,
The family is furnished with clothing complete."

" But when Ned has got through with the clothing, and when
He has thrown it aside — what d'ye do with it then?"

" Why, once more we go round, the circle complete,
And begin to use it for patches for Pete."

UNCLE EBEN'S CONSERVATISM.

UNCLE EBEN was careful in all that he said,
 He was never pronounced and dogmatic;
If he was as mad as a hornet at bay,
He couldn't be sure and emphatic.
He thought it was best to go sure and go slow,
And always take time for his whiskers to grow,
And his blame or his praise would end with this phrase:
" I dunno as I know; I dunno."

When his neighbors grew wild in political strife,
And asked his opinion about it — " I dunno but it is, I dunno but it ain't,"
He would slowly declare; " but I doubt it." Then he'd pause a long time, scratch
his head and lay low, For it took quite a while for his language to flow,
But at length he would say, in a calm kind of way:

" I dunno as I know; I dunno."
You might pelt him with truth, you might stone him with facts,
You could crush him with strong demonstration,
And teachers and preachers and lawyers could talk, —
He would have just the same hesitation;
He would still scratch his head, undecided and slow,
But no flush of conviction his face would o'erflow,
But slowly he'd say, in his old chronic way :
" I dunno as I know; I dunno."

"I dunno as I know, I dunno as I know
The refrain of his song of existence.
But we loved the old fellow—after he died
And his soul wandered off in the distance.
Then we thought, were we wiser and less fond of show,
Less weak and less proud of our work here below,
Like him we would say every day, every day:
u I dunno as I know; I dunno."

TWO FRIENDS.

I LIVED alone within a mighty city,
The crowds that come and go;
'Mid all its throngs, the foolish and the witty,
I had no friend or foe.

There were two men, within that mighty city,
Came to me from the throng;
One loved me with a love akin to pity,
The other's hate was strong.

The lover and the hater dwelt beside me,
Passed through the selfsame gate;

And neither, in their passing-by, denied me
The look of love or hate.

So many months within that mighty city
I loved my friend full well;
But him, my foe, for him I felt no pity—
But the deep hate of hell.

One morning, in the twilight, o'er the city
There came an icy breath:
My friend had passed beyond my love and pity,
The border-land of death.

Then was I lonely, and the way grew dreary;
I grimly fought with fate,
And cherished, with my loneliness aweary,
Dead love and living hate.

I sought his grave to whom my heart was mated—
My friend, the good and brave;
And there I saw the form of him I hated,
Bent, weeping, o'er his grave.

And then he told me that, in all the city,
But me and him below,
From all the throngs that needed God's sweet pity,
He had no friend or foe.

And now we live within the selfsame city,
No other friends we crave;
Our love is strong that sprang from human pity,
Above the dead man's grave.

EMERSON CORRECTED

A MAN named Em'son, so they say,
Got off a purty thing one day,
About a chap—I don't know who—
Who "builded better than he knew.
" In spite of Em'son, now, I swan,
He was built on a cur'us plan,
Accordin' to a strange idee
Thet don't at all resemble me;
In spite of all that I can do
I've builded worser than I knew.

I was a young and lazy lout,
But had my palace all planned out;
Its beauties never can be told-»-
Rosewood, mahogerny and gold;
It was a scrumptious sight to see
With all its gilt an' filigree.
But my real house scarce stops the rain,
An' has an old hat in the pane;
I did the best that I could do,
But builded worser than I knew.

I used to build my stately ships
An' launch 'em gran'ly from the slips,
An' in my dreams did I behold
Their freight of ivery an' gold.
Oh, they swep' gran'ly roun' the Horn,
An' rode the ocean like a swan.

But the real ship I set afloat

Was nothing but a leaky boat,
Without the scantest thread er sail—
I bale it with an ol' tin pail;
But for a fishing smack 'twill do.
I builded worser than I knew.

Yes, Mr. Em'son, very few
Have builded better than they knew;
Tis ten to one, howe'er we watch,
We'll make a bungle an' a botch.
It ain't because I don't know how,
To set the beams from stern to bow,
But my han' trembles so, I vum,
I cannot get the timbers plumb;
An' so it is, my life all through,
I've builded worser than I knew.

THE ELDER'S SERMON.

OUR elder told us yesterday, we had not learned to live
Until we learned how blessed 'tis to pardon and forgive ;
The dear, sweet, precious words he spake like heavenly manna fell;
The perfect peace they brought our hearts no human words can tell.

" Love brings millennial peace," he said; and, though my lips were dumb,
I still kept shouting in my soul, " Amen," and " Let it come ! "
" When men forgive all other men, the year of jubilee
Will dawn upon the world," he said. I said, " So let it be."

" So love your neighbor as yourself," he then begun again,
And Silas Fitz, across the aisle, he shouted out, " Amen! "

What right had he to yell " Amen," the low-toned measly hound!
Who took my cow, my new milch cow, and locked her in the pound!

The low-down, raw-boned, homely crank, a lunkhead and a lout,
Whose love and grace and heart and soul have all been rusted out —
To sit there in the sanctuary and holler out " Amen !"
If I could choke the rascal once he'd never shout again!

One day his dog came by my house : I called the brute inside,
Gave him a chunk of meat to eat, and he crawled off and died.
He just crawled off and died right then. Says I, " I'll let him see,
No long-legged simpleton like him can get the best of me."
But, oh, that sermon! — I would love to hear it preached again,
About forgiveness, charity and love of fellow men.
I should have felt as if I basked in Heaven's especial smile,
If that blamed villain, Silas Fitz, hadn't sat across the aisle.

SHORTEM SHY AND HERBERT SPENCER.

SHORTEM SHY plays round my knee
While I read Herbert Spencer,
But still the more I read and read,
My ignorance grows denser;
For Shortem Shy decries my taste,
And tells me every minute,
" Say, papa, I don't like that book,
There ain't no lions in it."

Now Herbert Spencer is a great,
A world-compelling thinker;
No heavy plummet line of truth
Goes deeper than his sinker.
But one man reads his work way through

For thousands that begin it,
They leave one-half the leaves uncut —
"There ain't no lions in it."

The age-old errors in their den
Does Herbert Spencer throttle,
And ranks with Newton, Bacon, Kant,
And ancient Aristotle.
The mighty homage of the few—
These towering giants win it;
The millions shun their hunting-ground, —
"There ain't no lions in it."

I leave this metaphysic swamp,
Thick grown with sturdy scions,
And roam the Meadows of Romance
With Shortem and his lions.
He brings his gaudy Noah's Ark book
And begs me to begin it;

" Better than Hubbut Pencer book,
That ain't no lions in it.
" Now wead about the efalunt
So big he scares the people;
An' wead about the kangerwoo
Who jumps up on the 'teeple."

So I take up the Noah's Ark book
And sturdily begin it,
And read about the " efalunts "
And lions that are in it.

Shortem will grow in soberness,

His life become intenser,
Some day he'll drop his " efalunts "
And take up Herbert Spencer.
But life can have no happier years
Than glad years that begin it,
And life sometimes grows dull and tame
That has no lions in it.

SOMETIME ORUTHER.

I KINDER suppose that we oughter to be good
To-day, an' this hour an' this very minute;
We oughter be perfect; I s'pose thet we would,
If it warn't sich a pesky hard thing to begin it.
But we're goin' to wheel right about face bimeby,
An' all of our weaknesses thoroughly smother;
Never cuss nor deceive, never swindle nor lie —
To-morrer, or nex' day, or sometime oruther!

An' we're goin' to wear all sorts uv jewels an' things,
An' biled shirts, an' stiff dickeys, an' them sort of duds,
An' tall hats an' thin butes, an' gre't big di'mon' rings,
An' live in a five-story house like blue bluds;
An' we're goin' to hev pie — and three times a day,—
An' pass aroun' all kines er sass to each other,
An' eat between meals jest w'enever we may—
To-morrer, or nex' day, or sometime oruther !

An' we won't work ernuff to get up a sweat
In the good time thet's comin', we'll jest loll and lean,
Stretch out in the shade with our lazy eyes shet,
An' hev our big tater crop dug by machine.
An' we won't do no things thet we don't want to do,

An' only jest do the things thet we druther,
An' the work that we'll do will be tarnally few —
To-morrer, or nex' day, or sometime oruther!

WAITING FOR THE MAIL.

WITH anxious features, worn and pale,
He waits the coming of the mail.
Each day he asks with hope and fear,
"My letter, is my letter here?"
Each day the answer strikes him dumb,—
"Not yet, old man; it has not come."
The harmless madman, old and gray,
No one would jeer or drive away. "
Ahme!" he sighs, "long years have passed,
But it will come, 'twill come at last."
And so he waits, in silence dumb,
The letter that will never come.

Through misty visions of his tears
He sees the long, far-sundered years;
The past comes up before him there —
When he was strong and she was fair;
Once more he feels, in very truth,
The leaping pulses of his youth;
A strong, strange joy he feels again,
The old wild fever in his brain;
An angry word, a careless tone,—
Then fifty weary years alone.
So long he waits, in silence dumb,
The letter that will never come.

Alas ! his poor old wits are fled,

He cannot know that she is dead;
And so he asks it o'er and o'er,
The same old question as before.
He wakes with morning light to say, "
My letter, it will come to-day !"
With tottering limbs that almost fail,
He creeps each morning to the mail,
And hears, with ever new regret,—
" Not yet, old man; not yet, not yet."
And then he waits, in silence dumb,
The letter that will never come.

Ah me ! poor madman, even we
Are dupes of fickle destiny;
In careless hope we waiting sit
For missives that were never writ;
We wait to see the harvest grown
From seed that we have never sown;
We seek the harbor mouth to hail
The vessels that will never sail;
We wait to see our garners filled
With fruit of fields we have not tilled;
We wait, in gathering stillness, dumb,
For letters that will never come !

PETER'S QUESTIONS.

WHEN Peter was a sturdy lad
He moved from Grassvale with his dad;
And left behind him Joe and John,
And little Jake and Jefferson;
Four chums of his by day and night
With whom he used to play and fight.

Now where is Joe, and where is John,
And where is Jake and Jefferson?

Ten years passed by and Pete came back
With these four questions in his pack:
" Now where is Joe, and where is John,
And where is Jake and Jefferson?" "
Joe digs his livin with his pick,
An' John keeps store down to the ' Crick';
Jake is away to school, I think,
An' Jefferson has took to drink."

And Pete came back in ten years more
With the same questions as before:
" Now where is Joe, and where is John, And
where is Jake and Jefferson?"
"Joe caught cold ditchin' in the rain,
An' — we shan't see poor Joe again;
An' John is rich, an' Jake is wise,
An' Jeff a scamp whom all despise."

In ten years Peter comes once more,
And asking questions as before :
" Now tell me where is old friend John,
And where is Jake and Jefferson?"
"Why, John he died a millionnaire;
Jake's gone to Congress, I declare.
An' Jeff—the poor old worthless scamp,
Is nothin' but a common tramp."

And once more, ten years later on,
He asks: " Where's Jake and Jefferson? "
"Hain't heard how Governor Jacob died?

He was the state's especial pride,
An' to his solemn funeral grand
The great men came from all the land;
But Jeff—it's no good to bewail—
Why poor old Jeff has gone to jail."

And once more, ten years later on,
Does Peter ask for Jefferson.
"Why hain't you heard the story yit?
The papers they was full of it,
It filled the land from side to side,
The way the poor old fellow died—
The Jeff who played with you when young,
The worthless, gray-haired Jeff, was hung."

Ten years are gone with days that were,
Gone questioner and answerer,
And with his questions comes no more
The gray-haired Peter as before.
Do well or ill your livelong task,
The time will come when none will ask,
" Now where is Joe, and where is John,
And where is Jake and Jefferson?"

THE LAND OF THE LEFT.

THE big thoughts that we thought, but could not ex-press;
The laws we proposed, but never enacted;
The love that we felt, but never confessed;
The business we planned, but never transacted;
The warp that we wove and neglected the weft, —
Are piled mountain high in the Land of the Left;
They are piled up so high That they graze the blue sky,

And burden the earth in the Land of the Left.

There is piled bottled thunder that never has burst,
There is stored livid lightning that never has struck,
And there stands the Last who had hoped to be First,
The lazy and luckless believer in luck;
And the hopes of which we all our lives were bereft,
Stalk proudly and grand thro' the Land of the Left;
And our gay dreams are there Looking wondrously fair
On the moonshiny strand of the Land of the Left.

And the office we run for, that evermore skips
From our grasp, like a shadow, we'll catch in that clime —
For there cabinet portfolios and postmasterships
Are thick as mosquitoes in camp-meeting time.
For Salt River cargoes of wonderful heft
Are dumped on the wharves of the Land of the Left;
There the office we prize
Will materialize —
We will find it at last in the Land of the Left.

Men left out in the cold will be pulled in to warm
Who all their lives long have chattered and shivered,
And their cargoes from Spain will sail in from the storm,
And the " letter they long for" be duly delivered.
It will come safe and sound, with its seal still uncleft,
From the postmaster's hands of the Land of the Left —
With a certified check That is worth a good speck
On the National Bank of the Land of the Left.

THE SILLICKMAN.

THERE'S var'us questions floatin' roun' 'bout how my life began,

An' how I clum feme's dizzy height an' now am sillick-man;
An' for the young men of the Ian', who after me shall come,
I want to tell the story of the way that I have clum.

I once was jest as poor an' mean an' miser'ble as you,
Et grub ez poor, wore duds ez mean ez all you fellers do;
But my " indomitable will," ez the reporter said,
An' my "untiring energy " hez brung me out ahead.

I saved my money, et corn bread, jest ez a cow eats grass,
An' I never used no butter, an' I never sighed for sass;
" Tough vittles for a workin' man? " Well, you must un'erstan'
If you think too much of fodder, w'y, you can't be sillickman.

I never tried to be no dood, wore overalls about,
An' w'en the outside got worn thin I turned 'em wrong side out;
Seven thirty-five a year for clo'es—this was my reg'lar plan—
An' now I'm reaping my reward — for I am sillickman.

I stored my min' 'ith useful facts, I read the **County Blow,** —
I borried it of neighbor Neal, didn't cost a cent, you know.
The **Grassvale Banner** is a sheet thet's full of spunk an' vim—
An' neighbor Nason took it, an' I borried it of him.

So I et my humble vittles, an' I 'conomized my time,
An' I stuffed myself with knowledge, an it never cost a dime.
Now you see I wear a biled shirt, lug a pencil in my han',
An' I set an' rule the people, for I now am sillickman.

An' I think it is my duty to tell what I have done,
An' jest the way I done it, to my feller countrymun.
For the young men of the country who after me shall come,
I now have told the story of the way that I have clum.

THE PIONEER.

JIM CROKER lived far in the woods, a solitary place,
Where the bushes grew, like whiskers on his unrazored face;
And the black bear was his brother and the catamount his chum,
And Jim he lived and waited for the millions yet to come.
Jim Croker made a clearing, and he sowed it down with wheat,
And he filled his lawn with cabbage, and he planted it with beet,
And it blossomed with potatoes and with peach and pear and plum,
And Jim he lived and waited for the millions yet to come.

Then Jim he took his ancient axe and cleared a forest street,
While he lived on bear and succotash and young opossum meat,
And his rhythmic axe strokes sounded, and the woods no more were dumb,
While he cleared a crooked highway for the millions yet to come.

Then they came like aimless stragglers, they came from far and near,
A little log-house settlement grew round the pioneer;
And the sound of saw and broadaxe made a glad industrial hum, Jim said,
"The Coming Millions, they have just begun to come."

And a little crooked railway curved round mountain hill and lake,
Crawling toward the forest village, like an undulating snake;
And one morn the locomotive puffed into the wilderness,
And Jim said, "The Coming Millions, they are coming by
express."

And the village grew and prospered, but Jim Croker's hair was grayer;
When they got a city charter and old Jim was chosen mayor,.
But Jim declined the honor, and moved his household goods
Far away into the forest, to the old primeval woods.

Far and far into the forest moved the grizzled pioneer,
There he reared his hut and murmured, " I will build a city here."
And he hears the wood-fox barking, and he hears the partridge drum,
And the old man sits and listens for the millions yet to come.

WOODCHUCKING.

I HAVE chased fugacious woodchucks over many leagues of land,
But at last they've always vanished in a round hole in the sand;
And though I've been woodchucking many times — upon my soul —
I have never bagged my woodchuck, for he always found his hole.

But 'tis fun to go woodchucking when a fellow is a boy,
When all muscular exertion is exhilarating joy,
Though you can't get near the woodchuck so's to touch him with a pole,
And the evanescent rascal always slides into his hole.

How I chased the panting fugitive and raised the battle cry,
With a vision right before me of a chunk of woodchuck pie;
With a vision right before me of this culinary goal,
Did I reach to grab my woodchuck — and he vanished in his hole.

And I often go woodchucking — I have chased him here and there —
That lank, fugacious woodchuck, like a long streak through the air;
For the projects I have followed, as I neared the eager goal,
Have made themselves invisible, and vanished in their hole.

I have chased my hot ambitions through the meadow, white with flowers,
Chased them through the clover blossoms, chased them through the orchard bowers,
Chased them through the old scrub pastures till, with weariness of soul,
I at last have seen them vanish, like a woodchuck in his hob.

But there's fun in chasing woodchucks; and I'll chase the vision still,
If it leads me through the dark pine woods, and up the stony hill;
There's a glorious expectation that still lingers in my soul,
That some day I'll catch that woodchuck ere he slides into his hole.

DIVORCE.

WHEN two nags won't hitch together, but balk an' raise a rumpus,
An' bite, an' throw their feet aroun' to all pints uv the compass,
Them hosses I don't drive no more, attached to the same kerridge —
An' I have jest the same idee about divorce an' merridge.

A man an' wife should live in peace, the nateral way of livin',
In one long holiday of luv, an' honor an' thanksgivin';
But w'en they learn to hate each other, an' live a life of snarlin',
An' " wretch " it takes the place of " dove," an' " brute " the place of " darlin',
";

W'en home becomes a battlefield. a scene of fight an' scrim-mage;
W'en luv pulls down her household gods, an' hate sets up his image;
An w'en no power in heaven or earth can take the pair an' mate 'em —
It's time for the divorce court, then, to come an' separate 'em.

"But how about the baby, hey, the blameless little prattler?"
W'y, in a nest of rattlesnakes, each snake becomes a rattler;
An' if you want the child to mix with gentlemen an' ladies,
It won't improve his chances much to be brought up in Hades.

DIVORCE.

Wen his father an his mother fight, it's better for the baby
To be brought up by charity, than be brought up where they be. "

But they should never wed again ! " I'm sorry to deny it,
But if a feller blunders once, w'y, let him rectify it.

But if all the men were jest like me', an* all their wives like
Molly, An' all the little boys like Dick, an' all the girls like Polly, —
W'y, all divorce courts would starve out, an each divorce attorney
Would pack his grip for happier climes, an' start upon his journey.

AN UNAMBITIOUS MAN.

NO hot ambition, wild and wan,
Deforms my life so fair,
I'd like to be a selectman,
And have folks call me "squire ";
But I'd not climb the topmost height,
Fame's fickle zephyr's sport,
But yet 'twould be no more than right,
I went to General Court; And so
I'd live and die content
In modest, shy retirement.

Tis true, I may move into town
Before my hair is grayer,
And then I hope to gain renown
And be elected mayor;
But I would not be grand and great
To make the people stare,
But were I governor of the state,
I think I would not care,
Nor let Fame's tempest-torn control
Mar my sweet quietude of soul.

I'd live the most content of men,

Far from Fame's maddening roar,
And could I go to Congress then,
I think I'd ask no more.
Of course the President must be
The man the people choose,
And should the people turn to me,
I could not well refuse.
But still ambition would not harm
My soul's serene, transcendent calm.

I wish no splendor when I die,
But all things neat and plain,
A catafalque of ebony,
A six mile funeral train;
And I would rest in peace content,
If my loved land should raise
A million-dollar monument,
To speak to future days.
Let others toil and strain for fame,
I am content without a name.

THE UNPARDONABLE SIN.

I CAHN'T endure the stoopid, wude,
Unculchawed chap — the vulgar boah,
Who wears in the mawhning the same pair of twousers
He woah the day befoah. It makes me mad and vewy cwoss,
With pain and gwief I almost woah,
To see the next mawhning the same pair of twousers
He woah the day befoah !

And when I mingle with the thwong,
Down to the club or on the stweet,

It makes me fwantic that a man
Can be so doocid indiscweet,
So wough and weckless and so wude;
I weally want to spill his goah,
When he weahs in the mawhning the same pair of twousers
He woah the day befoah !

Now there are deeds I cahn excuse,
And wongs I cahn forgive,
But such a cwiminal as this
Shouldn't be allowed to live !
Why, the ideah ! the monstwous wetch
With wage and fuwy makes me woah,
Who wears in the mawhning the same pair of twousers
He woah the day befoah !

A FALL FROM GRACE.

WE alius uster to think Joe Bean a fairish sorter man,
W An' built upon a purty plumb an' perpendic'lar plan;
We made him sillickman an' squire, sent him to General Court;
Whatever post of trust he had he alius held the fort.

We sought a guvernor last year, we scoured the state through clean,
We couldn't find no better man, an' pounced on neighbor
Bean. I nomernated him myself, — yes, yelled out loud and plain:
" I nomernate old Joseph Bean—a man without a stain ! "

An' then the big convention roared, hurrahed, an' clapped an' yelled;
It took the cheerman half an hour afore the noise was quelled.
You'd think, the way they yelled and roared and pounded there like sin,
Joe Bean he was a perfect man an' angel Gabriel's twin.

But nex' day the papers hinted that his mother starved to death,
An' Joe wouldn't give her food enough to keep her mortal breath;
An' then another paper said he uster beat his wife,
An' how she hid out in the barn that she might save her life.

They said he was an infidel, an anarchist an' snide,
An' said it looked suspicious that ar way his father died;
An' then they said the hoss he driv should pain his guilty soul —
It looked exactly like the hoss Ned Butterfield had stole.

They said Ned Jones, the pedlar, found murdered on the green,
The last time he was seen alive was seen with Joseph Bean;
They said the Baptis' meet'n house burned to the ground last
May Was lighted by a certain man — but they didn't like to say.

But Joe was 'lected guvernor, an' now he rules the state,
But he wont never be the same to me, I calkerlate;
I uster think him honest, an' pure, an' jest, an' good, But now
I'm kinder 'shamed to live in the same neighbor¬hood.

THE TRUNDLE-BED VALLEY.

L KNOW a little valley, in among the mountains hid,
I A trundle bed for Natur's babes with grass green coverlid,
All buttoned down 'ith tulips, an' all trimmed 'ith dande¬lion,
A crib for Natur's child, like me, to toddle to an' lie on.

I love to watch the coverlid sewed with the lily's stem,
An' the trout brook is its bindin' thet curves way aroun' its hem.
Wen the burden is too heavy fer my heart an' han' an' head,
I jest choke down my tired sobs an' seek my trundle bed.

Four big mountains are its bed posts; down through its awning high,

The sun shines like a breas'-pin in the buzzom of the sky,
An' it shines so warm an* frien'ly where my coverlid is spread
Thet I don't need any candle w'en I seek my trundle-bed.

Mother Natur' loves her child'en, so the good ol' soul has spread
Tiger-lily tangled bed-quilts over my big trundle bed.
An' to give her fretful youngster no excuse for being cross,
She has stuffed a lazy pillow with the softest kind of moss.

So, w'en I'm torn an' tired do my weary footsteps tread
Up the pussy-wilier valley to my little trundle bed,
Mother Natur' bends her face down, and she seems to love me so
Thet I rise an' toddle bravely, all the way I have to go.

GOD-BE-GLORIFIED JONES' MORTGAGE.

HE bought in 1665 a farm of stumps and stones,
 His name was God-Be-Glorified, his surname it was Jones,
He put a mortgage on the farm, and then, in conscious pride,
" In twenty years I'll pay it up," said God-Be-Glorified.

The mortgage had a hungry maw that swallowed corn and wheat;
He toiled with patience night and day to let the monster eat;
He slowly worked himself to death, and on the calm hillside
They laid, beyond the monster's reach, good God-Be-Glorified.

And the farm with its incumbrances of mortgage, stumps and stones
It fell to young Melchizedek Paul Adoniram Jones.
Melchizedek was a likely youth, a holy, godly man,
And he vowed to raise that mortgage like a noble Puritan.

And he went forth every morning to the rugged mountain side,
And he dug, as dug before him, poor old God-Be-Glorified;

He raised pumpkins and potatoes down the monster's throat to pour;
He gulped them down and smacked his jaws, and calmly asked for more.

He worked until his back was bent, until his hair was gray —
On the hillside through a snowdrift they dug his grave one day!
His first-born son, Eliphalet, had no time to weep and brood,
For the monster by his doorstep growled forever for his food.

He fed him on his garden truck, he stuffed his ribs with hay,
And he fed him eggs and butter, but he would not go away;
And Eliphalet he staggered with the burden, and then died
And slept with old Melchizedek and God-Be-Glorified.

Then the farm it fell to Thomas, and from Thomas fell to John,
Then from John to Eleazur, but the mortgage still lived on;
Then it fell to Ralph and Peter, Eli, Absalom and Paul,
Down through all the generations — but the mortgage killed them all!

About a score of years ago, the farm came down to Jim —
And Jim called in the mortgagee and gave the farm to him.
There's no human heart so empty that it has no ray of hope,
So Jim gave up the ancient farm and went to making soap.

He grew a fifty-millionnaire, a bloated, pampered nature.
He owned ten railroads, twenty mines, the whole State legislature,
And thousands did his gruff commands, and lived upon his bounty;
And he came home, bought back the farm, and the entire county.

THE QUARTET'S ANTHEM.

OH yes, I heerd the anthem sung by thet big church quartet,
My wife she raved about it, but I kep' my own mouth shet; "
No sweeter song," she sed, " is sung by any angel's lip " ;

An' I sot still an' heerd her talk, an' never raised a yip.

They sang, " We shall be changed; " that's all; that's all, or purty nigh;
"We shall be changed,—we shall be changed,—we shall be changed." Says I,
" If you perpose all day an' night jest them same words to sing,
W'y I should think a change would be a very proper thing."

The tenor sang "We shall be changed;" an' then struck in the bass,
Who sang, " We shall, we shall be changed " from the bottom of his face;
The alto and soprano then both tried their vocal range,
An' both emphatically expressed the certainty of "change."

The absence of idees wuz drowned in plenteousness of voice.
What strict econermy of words, an' 'stravagance of noise !
For they were stingy of their words and generous of their strains,
An' they were spendthrifts of their lungs an' misers of their brains.

An' they call this mighty music; 'taint for me to say it's not;
But I think music's better w'en its slightly mixed with thought;
I think yer lungs give forth to men a more inspirin' strain
If they first have made connection with the engine of yer brain.

W'en Maria rocked our boy to sleep an' sung her baby song
That quiet Sabbath evenin', with the shadders growin' long,
"The music of thet baby song," sez I to her, sez I,
"It beats yer quartet anthem out, an' knocks the thing sky high!"

HE WANTED TO KNOW.

HE wanted to know how God made the worl'
Out er nothin' at all,
W'y it wasn't made square, like a block or a brick,
Stid er roun', like a ball,

How it managed to stay held up in the air,
An' w'y it don't fall;
All sich kin' er things, above an' below,
He wanted to know.

He wanted to know who Cain had for a wife,
An' if the two fit;
Who hit Billy Patterson over the head,
If he ever got hit;
An' where Moses wuz w'en the candle went out,
An' if others were lit;
If he couldn' fin' these out, w'y his cake wuz all dough,
An' he wanted to know.

An' he wanted to know 'bout original sin;
An' about Adam's fall;
If the snake hopped aroun' on the end of his tail
Before doomed to crawl,
An' w'at would hev happened if Adam hedn' et
The ol' apple at all;
These ere kind er things seemed ter fill him 'ith woe,
An' he wanted to know.

An' he wanted to know w'y some folks wuz good,
An' some folks wuz mean,
W'y some folks wuz middlin' an' some folks wuz fat,
An' some folks wuz lean,
An' some folks were very learned an' wise,
An' some folks dern green;
All these kin' er things they troubled him so
That he wanted to know.

An' so he fired conundrums aroun',

For he wanted to know;
An' his nice crop er taters 'ud rot in the groun',
An' his stuff wouldn't grow,
For it took so much time to ask questions like these,
He'd no time to hoe;
He wanted to know if these things were so,
Course he wanted to know.

An' his cattle they died, an his horses grew sick,
'Cause they didn't hev no hay;
An' his creditors pressed him to pay up his bills,
But he'd no time to pay,
For he had to go roun' askin' questions, you know,
By night an' by day;
He'd no time to work, for they troubled him so,
An' he wanted to know.

An' now in the poorhouse he travels aroun'
In just the same way,
An' asks the same questions right over ag'in,
By night and by day;
But he haint foun' no feller can answer em' yit,
An' he's ol' an' he's gray,
But these same ol' conundrums they trouble him so,
That he still wants to know.

A GREAT CONTROVERSIALIST.

Do fact Uncle Jonas would take upon trust,
He would cavil and question and doubt it,
 And would say to each logical dogmatist's thrust,
" Waal, now, let us arger about it."
Every" p'int " of the question he'd marshal with care,

And march all around and about it,
And say, while he stroked his last vestige of hair,
" Waal, now, let us arger about it"

On faith, on predestination and grace,
On election, and foreordination
He'd " arger" all day without ever a trace
Of exhaustion or disinclination.
When the the pastor advised him to think of his sins,
"You're a sinner," he said, " none can doubt it,"
It brought Uncle Jonas at once to his pins,
" Waal, now, let us arger about it."

And when he was married and led his young bride
Right up to the church and the altar,
His mind didn't seem to be just satisfied,
Even then he was ready to falter.
"Do you take this young woman to be your own wife?"
Uncle Jonas was ready to doubt it;
" Do you take her for better or worse, and for life ? "
Said Jonas, " Let's arger about it."

Last week Uncle Jonas was fatally ill
In the very last stage of consumption,
His work was laid down at the farm and the mill
Without ever a hope of resumption.
" You must die," said the doctor; " the presence of death
Hovers o'er you, and no one can doubt it,
" But Jonas replied with his very last breath,
" Waal — now — let — us — arger—about — it."

And I fancy his soul up at Paradise gate,
And "argering" there at the portal,

While the hymns of the angels, in rapture elate,
Float over the city immortal.
Should the porter refuse him admittance therein,
Uncle Jonas would not go without it,
But his voice would rise up o'er the music's wild din,
"Naow, Peter, let's arger about it."

THE SPARE ROOM.

OUR front room, it was furnished fair,
But closed to all the life of home;
A reservoir of mouldy air,
A corpseless catacomb.
A stern domestic quarantine
Scared childish footsteps from its door,
As if a powder magazine
Were kept beneath the floor.

But when our folks had company,
The unused doors were opened wide,
And on the lavish luxury
We feasted open-eyed.
But we were strangers there, and hence
A nervous terror flushed each cheek;
Before the grand magnificence
We dared not move or speak.

And so we sat in vague alarms,
And sighed for some supporting pegs
For our unnecessary arms
And our superfluous legs;
We smiled our india-rubber smile, —
A long, perfunctory, muscular grin,

Which advertised to all outside
How bad we felt within.

Our hearts were in the barn at play,
Or played at tag about the shed;
Our bodies, statuettes of clay,
Sat in the parlor — dead.
In moveless suffering we sat on
And wept for back-yard haunts to roam,
As, by the brooks of Babylon,
The Hebrews wept for home.

In intellectual kitchens dole
Strong men their choicest life away,
And keep the front rooms of the soul
Unopened to the day.
They keep the pantry well-equipped,
The cellar they will never scant, —
The parlor is a darkened crypt
Without an occupant.

Hence, blest is he who quits the quest
For wealth, or fame's receding goal,
And every day returns for rest
To the front room of the soul.
Who lets the tempest rave and roll
Around him; in his glad release,
Within the front room of the soul
He findeth perfect peace.

ENOCH AND CYRUS AND JERRY AND BEN.

ENOCH and Cyrus and Jerry and Ben

Were babies together, four fat little men,
Four bald-headed babies who bumped themselves blue,
And sprawled, grabbed and tumbled, as all babies do.
Full of laughter and tears, full of sorrow and glee,
And big, bouncing bunglers, as all babies be.
All in the same valley lived these little men —
Enoch and Cyrus and Jerry and Ben.

Enoch and Cyrus and Jerry and Ben
Were fast little chums — till they grew to be men.
Eight bare little feet on the same errands flew
Thro' meadows besprinkled with daisies and dew ;
They were aimless as butterflies, thoughtless and free
As the summer-mad bobolink, drunken with glee.
A wonderful time were those careless days then
For Enoch and Cyrus and Jerry and Ben.

Enoch and Cyrus and Jerry and Ben
Grew from babies to boys, and from boys into men.
Too restless to stay in the circumscribed bound
Of the green hills that circled their valley around,
To the North and the South and the East and the West,
Each departed alone on a separate quest.
Ah, they'll ne'er be the same to each other again —
Enoch and Cyrus and Jerry and Ben.

Enoch and Cyrus and Jerry and Ben,
Companions in youth, were strangers as men;
Enoch grew rich and haughty and proud,
While Cyrus worked on with the toil-driven crowd;
In the councils of state Jerry held a proud place,
But Ben,' he sounded the depths of disgrace.
Ah, diverse were the lives of those boys from the glen —

Enoch and Cyrus and Jerry and Ben.

Enoch and Cyrus and Jerry and Ben, —
Who can read the strong fates that encompassed these men?
The fate that raised one to the summit of fame,
The fate that dragged one to the darkness of shame !
Ah, silence is best; neither glory nor blame
Will I grant to the honored or dishonored name.
We are all like those boys who grew to be men —
Like Enoch, or Cyrus, or Jerry, or Ben.

THE GOVERNOR'S FATHER.

ORTER be proud er Ned," yer say; "
One the bigges' men er the day;
He is a fav'rite son er fate
The bigges' gun in all the State."
Wall, arter all is said an' done
This 'ere smart man is my own son!
An' I — I alius dug the dirt,
An' alius wore an unbiled shirt;
Alius stubbed round in cowhide boots,
An' alius dressed in drillin' suits;
Oner be proud er him ?- Dear me !
I orter—wall—I guess I be !

Ned wuz a roly-poly kid,
An' jest the cutest things he did !
He jest slopped over with delight
An' spilt roun' sunshine day an' night!
Heaven's bung er happiness turned loose,
An' Ned he jest drunk in the joose;
He gurgled in his baby glee,

An' gosh ! he thought the worl'er me.
At night I tucked him in his bed
An' said, "I'm proud er little Ned."

An' Ned grew up, a likely lad,
An' hoed pertaters with his dad;
He spread the hay, an' milked the cow,
An' hoed the corn—I showed him how!
An' out here in the woods with me,
He bragged er what he hoped to be;
He said: "P'rhaps, sometime, I'll be great,
An' be the guv'nor of the State."
An' I sez : " Go ahead, my lad,
An' be an honor to yer dad."
But now he's grown to what you see,
But—wall—he's grown away from me.
Orter be proud er him? — Ah me !
I orter—wall—I guess I be.

Ned's brain is full er mighty things,
Sich thoughts as fill the skulls er kings,
Thoughts fer big dictionary words,
While I still think of creams an' curds,
Of hoein' taters, plantin' corn, Jest ez
I did when Ned wuz born.
No longer does my rosy lad
Think jest the same thoughts as his dad;
An' I mus be, I've often said,
A purty common man to Ned.
How distant in the past they be,
Them days when Ned looked up to me !
Orter be proud er him ? Dear me !
I orter— wall— I guess I be.

The worl' a mighty man hez won,
But I — wall — I have lost my son;
An' Fame may laff an' dance with joy —
I druther cry — I've lost my boy !
Orter be proud er him ? — Ah me !
I orter — wall — I guess I be.

INGIN SUMMER.

NATUR', the good old schoolmarm who pities our distress
She gives her children every year a little glad recess;
An' ol' gray-headed boys an' girls, they feel their hearts thaw out,
An' life flows on as music'ly as water from a spout.

An' now the Ingin summer time, 'ith all its rest, is here,
A piece of sweet meat stuck between the slices of the year;
A sorter reign er jubilee 'twixt snow an' thunder showers;
A chunk er sweetness sandwiched in between the frost and flowers.

The Prince of the Power of the Air goes off on his vacation,
The devil jest holds up a spell an' stops his aggervation;
An' Natur' an' the heart er man, unriled by heat or flood,
They jest lay back an' hol' their breath, an' feel that God is good.

Now w'en we breathe we just take in great gulps er happiness,
We drink the air, like apple juice, from Natur's cider-press;
It jest comes tricklin' down thro' space from heaven's great vats above,
An' fills our lungs 4th oxygin, an' slops our souls 'ith love !

I love my neighbor like myself, this Ingin summer day,
I feel it's glorious to live, for life is all O. K.
Natur', the good ol' schoolmarm who pities our distress,

She gives her children every year this little glad recess.

CHORES.

TED DORCUM always used to say
When we asked him to come and play
With us boys down to Harry More's, "
I've gotter to stay and do the chores."
No recreation would he take
For all his weight in jelly cake—
No glad fun in or out of doors;
He had to stay and do the chores.

We drove a woodchuck in the wall
But Jed he paid no heed at all;
A circus passed through Lower Town
But busy Jed he couldn't go down.
The elephant went tramping by
And shook the earth and touched the sky,
The tiger howls, the lion roars,—
Jed stays at home and does the chores.

Much like Jed Dorcum are we all
Who long for great things and do small;
We moil among the trivial sods
Within the gardens of the gods,
While the dark clusters hang above
Rich with the juice of life and love.
We cannot reach and pluck them down,
These fair pomegranates of renown,
Whose juice life's early hope restores,
For we must work and do the chores.

Above us sternly loom forever
The mighty Mountains of Endeavor,
And whoso on their summit stands
Looks on the sun-kissed table lands.
We grasp our mountain staff to climb
Their sky enshrouded peaks sublime,
Up where the crystal torrent pours —
And then we pause to do our chores.

We start with courage in the heart
To try the endlessness of art,
In hope that we may speak some day
The word the Spirit bids us say.
But e'er we speak the word aright
The shadows come and it is night.
Put out the light and close the doors,
For good or ill we've done our chores.

THE INKSTAND BATTLE.

WE are making smokeless powder
And big bombs to throw a mile,
That will blow the foe to chowder
In the true dynamic style.
Talk not of the bloody red man,
And the foe his arrow drops —
Every ball, it means a dead man,
Every bullet means a corpse

We've a whirling gun; you spin it
And the myriad bullets fly,
And a hundred men a minute
Roll their stony eyes and die.

" Make your swath of dead men deeper,"
Thus the modern Spirit saith, "
Start me up this rattling reaper
On the harvest fields of death."

Let us stop this wild death's revel!
Martin Luther, so 'tis said,
Threw his inkstand at the devil
And the black fiend turned and fled.
Smite your world-wrong; don't combat it
With a fusillade of lead;
Simply throw your inkstand at it ;
Come to-morrow: it is dead.

When the world upon the brink stands
Of some crisis steep and dread,
Like brave soldiers seize your inkstands,
Hurl them at the devil's head;
Pour your ink-pots in a torrent
Till the strangling demon sink,
Till the struggling fiend abhorrent
Drown in oceans of black ink.

For the man who's born a fighter,
For the brain that's learned to think,
There is dynamite and nitre
In a bottle of black ink.
Though it makes no weeping nations,
And it leaves no gaping scars,
Placed 'neath Error's strong foundations,
'Twill explode them to the stars.

SHE TALKED.

S HE talked of Cosmos and of Cause,
And wove green elephants in gauze,
And while she frescoed earthen jugs,
Her tongue would never pause:
On sages wise and esoteric,
And bards from Wendell Holmes to Herrick —
Thro' time's proud Pantheon she walked,
And talked and talked and talked and talked 1

And while she talked she would crochet,
And make all kinds of macrame,
Or paint green bobolinks upon
Her mother's earthen tray;
She'd decorate a smelling bottle
While she conversed on Aristotle;
While fame's proud favorites round her flocked,
She talked and talked and talked and talked !

She talked and made embroidered rugs,
She talked and painted 'lasses jugs,
And worked five sea-green turtle doves
On papa's shaving mugs;
With Emerson or Epictetus,
Plato or Kant, she used to greet us:
She talked until we all were shocked,
And talked and talked and talked and talked !

She had a lover, and he told
The story that is never old,
While she her father's bootjack worked

A lovely green and gold.
She switched off on Theocritus,
And talked about Democritus;
And his most ardent passion balked,
And talked and talked and talked and talked !

He begged her to become his own;
She talked of ether and ozone,
And painted yellow poodles on
Her brother's razor hone;
Then talked of Noah and Neb'chadnezzar,
And Timon and Tiglath-pileser —
While he at her heart portals knocked,
She talked and talked and talked and talked !

He bent in love's tempestuous gale,
She talked of strata and of shale,
And worked magenta poppies on
Her mother's water pail;
And while he talked of passion's power,
She amplified on Schopenhauer —
A pistol flashed: he's dead ! Unshocked,
She talked and talked and talked and talked !

THE RAIL AROUND THE JAIL.

DON'T you hold your head so high,
Or you'll bust holes in the sky;
When you walk, the big earth jars,
An' yer whiskers sweep the stars,
An' yer fill up the hull street,
Whirl the worl' roun' with yer feet,
An' refuse to speak to me —

Guess you don't know who I be.
So you won't say " howdy do,"
But I'm jest ez good ez you;
May hev less orig'nal sin,
If I hain't no diamond pin;
Ain't no line divides a man
From his fellers, understan';
Ain't no line except the rail
Of the fence aroun' the jail.

Ef I keep outside the rail
Of this fence aroun' the jail,
I'm a great gun, fit ter bang
In the big Four Hundred gang.
An' the president, understan',
Is but jest my hired man
An' I watch and boss w'ile he
Does the nation's chores for me.

What we're goin' to do bimeby,
'Fore the universe goes dry,
Is to make no diff'runce — see ?
'Twixt sich chaps ez you an' me;
One be jest ez good ez t'other,
Both in love 'ith one another:
Wile we keep outside the rail
Of the fence aroun' the jail.

You hain't got no bluer blood,
An' yer made er the same mud;
An' yer vittles, fresh or stale,
Comes from the same dinner-pail.
Thet's a good 'nough creed for me

Thet was taught in ol' Judee;
Men are bruthers; good enough;
Men are bruthers; thet's the stuff!

An' the time is goin' to be
Wen we'll come to thet idee,
Thet all men outside the rail
Of the fence aroun' the jail,
Will all mix like gin'ral dough,
An' love's yeast will make it grow;
An' by thet time Natur's cake
Will be riz enough to bake.

THE LAND OF GIT-THARE.

THERE are purple grapes in the Land of Git-Thare
Whose clusters climb higher and higher,
In each rounded breast is the vintage of rest
That tones the lax nerves with an infinite zest,
And thrills the dull brain with new fire.
Through musical rushes the streams flow along,
And the valleys resound with the Daughters of Song,
And flaunt with their floating attire;
There is shade, and cool fountains, and music to spare,
In the mountain-hemmed vales of the Land of Git-Thare.

And the branches bend down with pomegranates of peace,
That ooze with the juice of delight,
Through the odorous Pass of the Spangled Grass,
To the Lily-Pad Lake, that is clearer than glass,
Dream zephyrs float down from the height.
They are heavy with perfumes and odorous smells,
That rise from the grots of the Daffodil Dells

Where the noonday is mixed with the night.
There is perfume and song and sweet music to spare
In the verdurous vales of the Land of Git-Thare.

But you climb the tall mountains of Precipice Land
Ere you come to the Land of Git-Thare;
And you cross the White Land of Poisonous Sand
Till you reach the black shore of the Shipwreck Strand,
By the blood-red Sea of Despair.
And you sail this sea like a lonesome morass,
Till you come to the pass of the Spangled Grass,
And a strong-armed angel is there.
And a glittering sword in his hand gleams bare,
To drive back all who seek for the Land of Git-Thare.

THE CALF ON THE LAWN.

I'M goin' to hitch this 'ere young caff out here in my front lawn,
He'll stay right here an' chaw the grass 'till the hull thing is chawn,
He'll chaw thet corner off to-day, until he's et it bare;
Ter-morrer I will move his stake, an' he'll chaw over there.

Looks bad, yer say, to see a caff out in a man's front yard,
An' blattin', like a barn-yard, on this stylish boolevard:
But thet air caff shall eat thet grass until I get him fat,
An' if he feels like blattin', w'y, I reckon he will blat.

Wen I fust took my farm out here this was a country road,
Across the way was parstchure lan', where huckleberries growed;
My caff wuz then hitched in my yard fer the hull town's in-spection,
An' no darn, enterprisin' dood cum roun' to make objection.

Wen this road growed a village street, my caff was in the yard,

An' now the street it swells 'ith style — a city boulevard !
But I will hitch this ere young caff out here in my front lawn.
He'll stay right here an' chaw the grass till the hull thing is chawn.

You say the way I carry on makes the hull city laff;
Wall, let 'em laff, — this ere's my lawn, an' this ere is my caff,
An' things hez reached the purtiest pass the worl' hez ever sawn,
Ef an ol' duff can't let his caff chaw grass on his own lawn.

Wall, let 'em laff; this 'ere young caff shall stay here anyhow,
An' if I hear 'em laff too hard, I'll trot out the ol' cow;
I'll hitch 'em both to the same stake, right here in my front lawn,
An' let 'em stay an' chaw the grass till the hull thing is chawn !

SHORTEM'S QUESTION.

YOUNG SHORTEM he has much to learn,
And though he's round and fat,
He stubs to everything he sees
And points and says, " Wot's zat? "
The trees, the grass, the sticks, the stones,
The horse, the dog, the cat, —
They all are wonders of the world,
And so he asks "Wot's zat?"

Young Shortem sits upon my knee
And in my knowledge basks;
In my omniscient wisdom I
Can answer all he asks.
He thinks the fount of learning springs
From just beneath my hat;
He comes right to the fountain head
And asks and asks," Wot's zat ? "

We all are Shortems larger grown,
Who roam with curious eye,
And when we cease to say, " What's that?"
Why, then it's time to die.
Life's baffling, endless mystery—
We wonder much thereat;
Before the riddle of the world
We only say, " What's that?"

The sages of the elder world,
The thinkers of to-day,
All ask young Shortem's question in
The same old curious way.
A million worlds whirl round their view,
They wonder much thereat;
They stand in the immensities
And only ask, " What's that? "

The mighty serial goes on
With wonders manifold,
The story of the universe,
Will never all be told.
And through the great eternal years
We'll wonder much thereat,
Forever and forever ask,
"What's that? what's that? what's that?"

TELLIN' WHAT THE BABY DID.

IN the cosy twilight hid,
Tellin' what the baby did,
Sits Matilda every night,

Twixt the darkness an' the light,
Tells me in her cutest way
All the hist'ry of the day,
Gives me all; leaves nothin' hid,
Tellin' what the baby did.

Beats the whole decline an' fall
Of the Roman Empire.
Gol! William Shakspeare never hed
Cuter thoughts than baby said,
An' he hez, to sing his thoughts,
Sweeter words than Isaac
Watts. Tildy, she leaves nothin' hid,
Tellin' what the baby did.

Pooty hard schoolmarm is fate
To her scholars, small an' great;
I hev felt upon my han'
Tingle of her sharp rattan;
But she pities our distress,
An' she gives a glad recess
When Matilda sits, half hid,
Tellin' what the baby did.

Trudge off with my dinner pail
Every mornin' without fail;
Work, with hardly time for breath;
Come home, tired half to deatn;
But I feel a perfect rest
Settle down upon my breast,
Settin', by the twilight hid,
Hearin' what the baby did.

Sometimes I cannot resist,
An' I shake my doubled fist
In the face of fate and swear,
" You don't treat a fellow fair!"
Then, when I go home at night,
My whole system full of fight,
'Tildy, she sits there, half hid,
Tellin' what the baby did.

Then I jest make up with fate,
An' my happiness is great;
But if fate should lay its han'
On that baby, understand
Through the worl' I'd sulk apart
With red murder in my heart;
If she sat no more half hid,
Tellin' what the baby did.

HUSBAND AND HEATHEN.

O'ER the men of Ethiopia she would pour her cornu¬copia,
And shower wealth and plenty on the people of Japan,
Send down jelly cake and candies to the Indians of the Andes,
And a cargo of plum pudding to the men of Hindustan;
And she said she loved 'em so —
Bushman, Finn and Eskimo. —
If she had the wings of eagles to their succor she would fly,
Loaded down with jam and jelly, Succotash and vermicelli,
Prunes, pomegranates, plums and pudding, peaches, pine-apples and pie.

She would fly with speedy succor to the natives of Molucca
With whole loads of quail and salmon, and with tons of fricassee,
And give cake in fullest measure

To the men of Australasia
And all the archipelagoes that dot the Southern sea;
And the Anthropophagi,
All their lives deprived of pie,
She would satiate and satisfy with custard, cream and mince;
And those miserable Australians
And the Borrioboolaghalians,
She would gorge with choicest jelly, raspberry, currant, grape and quince.

But, like old war-time hardtackers, her poor husband lived on crackers
Bought at wholesale from a baker, eaten from the mantel shelf;
If the men of Madagascar
And the natives of Alaska,
Had enough to sate their hunger, let him look out for himself.
And his coat had but one tail
And he used a shingle nail
To fasten up his " gallus " when he went out to his work;
And she used to spend his money
To buy sugar plums and honey
For the Terra del Fuegian and the Turcoman and Turk.

THE RATTLE OF THE DOLLAR.

THE air it tastes like nectar oozed from heaven's own laboratory,
And the sunshine falls like ointment on the forehead of a king,
When a man feels in his pocket, flushed with full financial glory,
And he hears the nickles rattle, and hears the quarters ring.
Though winter storms assault his path, and drift his way and block it,
In his heart he feels the sunshine of an endless summer time,
For he listens to the music of the money in his pocket
To the rattle of the dollar and the jingle of the dime.
The famous violinists, And the fiddlers and cornettists,
And the mighty organ players Of every age and clime,

Make a slow and droning music, Full of discord and of jangle,
When you match it with the rattle,
With the rattle of the dollar and the jingle of the dime.

Then the star of hope arises, and in glittering ascendance,
It lights the rugged pathway and the labyrinth of gloom;
For we feel the swelling majesty of perfect independence;
And though the universe is large, we shout, "More room ! more room!"

The pangs of penury are hard, howe'er the sages talk it,
And poverty is perilous—the borderland of crime;
But there's courage in the clatter of the coin within your pocket,
In the rattle of the dollar and the jingle of the dime !
Like the music of King David
On the dulcimer and taber,
On the harp whose strings were many,
In that old melodious time,
Is the music of the clinking
Of the jolly halves and quarters,
And the ringing resonant rattle,
The rattle of the dollar and the jingle of the dime !

And the time we hope is coming when the millions and the masses
May hear this merry music with no interval between;
Life cease to be an endless quest for meal and for molasses,
And a long unanswered problem of coal and kerosene.
And we hear it in the distance — woe to him who tries to block it,
Tries to block the onward progress of the struggling march of time,
When all shall hear the music of the rattling of the pocket,
Hear the rattle of the dollar and the jingle of the dime.
And the patient wives and babies Shall not starve for lack of money,
Shall not dress in rags and tatters In that happy coming time;
For the world shall ring with music

Of a billion bulging pockets,
Each one ringing with the rattle—
With the rattle of the dollar and the jingle of the dime.

THE LAND OF NEVER WAS.

WHERE are all those shining valleys which we used to sing and rhyme,
Purple with the clustered fruitage of the harvest fields of time ?
Where are all those young ambitions, framed in rainbows, aureoled
With a halo mist of glory woven from the sunset's gold?
Gone before their realization, like effects without a cause,
Vanished in the misty limbo of the Land of Neverwas !

Where are all those toppling castles, turret-tipped with moon¬lit glows,
Gay with youths and laughing maidens, thro' their echoing porticoes?
Where are those aerial brownstones with their gargoyles of red mist,
Touched with sardonyx and topaz and with gold and amethyst ?
They have floated on the summer clouds that never wait nor pause,
Down below the dim horizon of the Land of Neverwas !

Where are all those golden galleons floating on the tideless seas,
With their sendal sails distended, bound for the Hesperides,
Sailing thro' the dashing dolphins, thro' the archipelagoes,
Where each wafted breeze is heavy with the cinnamon and rose?
Ah! their hulks have turned to shadow and their sails have turned to guaze,
And, like dream ships, they have vanished in the Land of Neverwas!

Tis the purple land of rainbows on an island for away,
None but little folks and babies 'neath its fronded branches stray;
Never does a bird of passage land upon its towering cliff.
But sometimes a daring poet sees it from his dream-blown skiff,
But when he tries to sing of it men neither heed nor pause,
For most men are disbelievers in the Land of Neverwas!

A PROSPEROUS COUPLE.

WALL, wife, it's fifty years ago sence you an' me wuz tied,
An' we hev clum the hills er life together side by side,
How we hev prospered, hain't we, wife? an' how well off we be ! —
W'en we wuz spliced we owned one cow, an' now, gosh, we own three.

I owed five Hundred on this farm, five hundred dollars then,
But I hev prospered far beyond the gen'l run er men.
A kindly Providence hez shaped the rough course of events,
An' now I owe four twenty-five an' thirty-seven odd cents.

'Twas only fifty years ago you only had one dress,
To aggervate your beauty and increase your loveliness;
Now you've got two scrumptious dresses, an' a most tre-mendous bonnet,
With a monst'ous horticult'ral fair a-flourishin' upon it.

Three chairs wuz in our sittin'-room but fifty years ago.
But we hev prospered wonderf''ly, an' now there's five, you know.
We've gained a lamp, a puddin' dish, an extra yoke er steers,
A grin'stone, an' a dingle cart, — an' all in fifty years !

It's all true w'at our pastor said, the worl' moves fast to-day,
An' with a quick, electric whiz goes spinnin' on its way;
It jest goes spinnin' on its way until its work is done,
But there's few spinners, my dear wife, who've spun ez we have spun.

HE CAME TO STAY.

HE entered the shop like a shaft from a bow,
And, " Here are some tickets," he said, " to the show,

And who are there here who proposes to go? "
" I," " I," cried the boss and the journeyman lad,
The sweet girl-accountant, the errand-boy bad;
"I," " I," cried the workmen — he gave all he had;
And a shout profound, in a tumult of sound,
Broke over his glorified head.

" And here is a bill I have brought to-day,
And who is the man I shall look to for pay ?
I would like it cleared up and out of the way.
" Not a sound was made, not a tone was heard,
Not a muscle moved, not a finger stirred,
And never a man spake a single word.
And stillness sate, like the presence of fate,
And a silence profound, for its absence of sound,
Was heard for miles and for leagues around
When he said, " I will sit down and wait."

SEBASTIAN MOREY'S POEM.

THE 'Lantic an New England, the Century an' Harper s,
Scribner's, an' all the rest uv 'em, is all a set er sharpers.
Wen they fin' a son er genuis an' a regular ten-strike poet,
An' a close chum er the muses, they hain't sense enough to know it.
I writ a roaring poem once an' I sent it to the 'Lantic,
Nex' mail, full chisel it come back an' nearly driv me frantic.
I sent it then to all the rest to see how they would find it,
But they with their durned printed slips "respectfully de¬clined " it.

Wen I got up that poem in a wild divine afflatus,
My hull brain was runnin' over liked a heaped-up hill er taters,
An' I rushed aroun' permiscus-like an' not at all partic'lar,
With my coat-tails horizontal an' my hair a perpendic'lar.

I tore aroun' in frenzy, like a dog that's taken pizen,
I feared I'd knock the stars out an' collide with the horizon,
For all out-doors warn't big enough fer ol' Sebastian Morey,
For I could shin a rainbow way up to the streets of glory.

It come out in the turnip patch, an' I, I seemed to waller
In an ocean uv forgetfulness until I couldn't swaller,
The bung to heaven's gret music box got loose an' out it bounded,
The music splashed an' spilt itself till I wuz nearly drownded.

Somehow I couldn't fin' room enough, I breathed gret gulps er glory,
An' all St. Peter's angels loafed aroun' Sebastian Morey;
The stars wuz makin' music an' their tones wuz more than middlin',
Each leaf er grass a fiddle string, an' every breeze a-fiddlin'!

My lips seemed wet 'ith frankincense an' honey mixed with nectar,
With the milk of human kindness thet don't need no milk in-spector ;
An' I felt the yeast of poetry workin' like a fiery leaven,
An' my arms swung roun' the firmament, my whiskers swep' the heaven.

W'y! all space wuz stuffed 'ith rainbows 4th gold pots fer me to capture,
An' all God's everlastin' hills wuz bustin' into rapture,
The birds, the frogs, the grasshoppers, all sung their loud hozanner,
An' every single fores' tree turned into a pianner.

The poem took me like the cramp: I felt my eyes a-bright-nin'
With a gran' celestial vision, w'en I winked they spurted lightnin';
I grabbed my pencil, crunched my teeth, an' terribly in earnes'
I jest threw off thet poem red-hot from the fiery furnace.

If there ever wuz a poem writ I hed a chance to git it,
All heaven wuz bilin' in my soul w'en I sot down an' writ it,

The angels tol' me every word, an' it would make me famous
If every tarnal editor warn't sich an ignoramus.

Wal, let 'em print their sappy stuff, but I can do without it,
I've shet off my subscription an' now let 'em squirm about it;
The 'Lantic an' New England the Century an' Harper's,
Scribner's an' all the rest uv 'em is all a setter sharpers.

THE SHAPE OF THE SKULL.

IS a man stupid, or brilliant or wise,
Surpassingly able or dull?
It all depends on his cranial bumps,
Depends on the shape of his skull;
And there are some things that some men cannot do,
Let them struggle and try till they're dead,
Unless they can build a big L on their brain
And alter the shape of their head.
Then do not attempt those impossible feats,
And struggle until you are gray,
On tasks for which you were never designed,
When your skull isn't shaped the right way.

For the world is filled with irrational men
Who struggle and try to attain
The cloud-bannered peaks of impossible heights,
Without the right bulge of the brain.
For the plastic skull of the man is shaped
By a fate that is greater than he,
And he must judge by the shape of his head
The trend of his destiny.
Then judge by the fit of your cranium case,
Don't squander your powers I pray,

In reaching for unattainable things
When your skull isn't shaped the right way.

THEY SLANT IN THAT DIRECTION.

TO tell w'y men is so an' so
Is much too hard for me,
It is the way the critters grow
Thet makes them what they be;
I only say the reason w'y
So many men is all awry,
An' full of imperfection,
Is simply jest because they can't
Git any other kind of slant —
They slant in thet direction.

I do not try to make it plain
W'y men are proud or meek,
Or with a mighty sweep er brain
Or vast expanse er cheek;
It is enough fer me to know
It is the way the critters grow
In every town an section;
There is some power thet gives a cant,
Some mighty "skid" thet makes 'em slant —
All slant in thet direction.

An' I don't blame men overmuch
An' on their vices rant,
Till I look up their traits an' such
To fin' the way they slant;
An' I won't smite 'em hip an' j'int
Until I find the way they p'int,

Nor scold each imperfection;
A little cherity I'll grant,
For men are bad because they slant—
They slant in thet direction.

TAKE yer head with yer," says ol' Uncle Joe,
Take yer head with yer wherever ye go,
Take yer head with yer, ye'll need it.
" Take yer heart with yer," says ol' Uncle Joe, "
Take yer heart with yer an' heed it;
Take yer heart with yer, wherever ye go,
Take yer heart with yer, ye'll need it.

" Let yer head and yer heart talk over the thing,
An' arger the case till they've tried it,
While you set in style like a judge or a king,
An' w'en they've stopped jawin', decide it."

THE TARIFF FIEND.

I TALKED to him of Jupiter and Dian,
The ancient gods who thronged Olympus' hill:
But he switched off on duties on pig iron,
And talked about McKinley's tariff bill.
He asked, the while I told of Troy and Homer,
What lowering of the tariff rates would do,
And what effect 'twould have upon Tacoma,
On Kankakee, Mauch Chunk and Kalamazoo;
Then talked about the duty on alpaca,
On turpentine, and tinfoil and tobacco.

Then I digressed upon predestination,
Talked Scripture, like a theologic dean,

He asked, if, in my candid estimation,
There shouldn't be higher rates on kerosene.
And then I talked of poetry and beauty —
He said all sections should together pull,
And if the East got hides exempt from duty,
The West should ask a higher rate on wool;
And if the sugar men should get a bounty,
So should the lumberers of Aroostook county.

I talked of Science probing earth and star,
Calm Science, by her handmaid Truth attended —
He said our present tariff rate on tar
At once should be materially amended.
I still talked Science, scattering error's mist,
Making the whole earth fairer and completer —
He said that salt should go on the free list
And so should sodium, soft soap and saltpetre.
And then he talked of tins and zincs and coppers,
Of revenues and European paupers.

I talked of history, literature, and art,
The thoughts of most inspired songs and sagas;
But when I stopped to breathe, he made a start
And said a tax should go on rutabagas.
I soothed him with a sentimental strain,
And told the joys of love and pure affection —
He said the rates for Michigan and Maine
Were not the rates for every other section.
I left him, and in smothered wrath went stalking;
When I returned next day he still was talking.

THE PRINCE'S BOW AND ARROWS.

THERE was a little Prince of Spain
Lived very long ago,
Who said the big horizon —
He would bend it like a bow.
His arrows in the form of ships
He'd shoot and make them go
To many undiscovered lands
Where gold and diamonds grow.
And so this little Prince of Spain
Longed for the years to go
Until his arm was strong enough
To bend his mighty bow.

And so this little Prince of Spain,
Like little boys you know,
As the advancing years went on
Did marvellously grow.
And he became the King of Spain
And made him ships to go
To many undiscovered lands
Where gold and diamonds grow.
His arrows in the form of ships
Swung idly to and fro,
For though his arm was very strong
He could not bend his bow.

We all are princes of the blood,
Who build our ships to go
To many undiscovered lands
Where gold and diamonds grow;

But still on old familiar seas
They wander to and fro,
And hug the immemorial shores
Where landward breezes blow.
And like the little Prince of Spain,
Who lived so long ago,
We have our arrows ready
But we cannot bend the bow.

DROP YOUR BUCKET WHERE YOU ARE.

OH, ship ahoy ! " rang out the cry, "
Oh, give us water or we die ! "
A voice came o'er the waters far,
"Just drop your bucket where you are."
And then they dipped and drank their fill
Of water fresh from mead and hill;
And then they knew they sailed upon
The broad mouth of the Amazon.

O'er tossing wastes we sail and cry "
Oh, give us water or we die ! "
On high, relentless waves we roll
Through arid climates for the soul;
'Neath pitiless skies we pant for breath
Smit with the thirst that drags to death,
And fail, while faint for fountains far,
To drop our buckets where we are.

Oh, ship ahoy ! you're sailing on
The broad mouth of the Amazon,
Whose mighty current flows and sings

Of mountain streams and inland springs,
Of night-kissed morning's dewy balm,
Of heaven-dropt evening's twilight calm,
Of nature's peace in earth or star —
Just drop your bucket where you are.

Seek not for fresher founts afar,
Just drop your bucket where you are;
And while the ship right onward leaps
Uplift it from exhaustless deeps;
Parch not your life with dry despair,
The stream of hope flows everywhere.
So, under every sky and star,
Just drop your bucket where you are.

MATILDA'S AND NATURE'S SPRING CLEANING.

I FIND the world, outside my house, is often all awry,
But my household is a model to direct the planet by,
Excepting in spring cleaning time — my home is then destroyed —
Tis made a primal chaos then, without a form and void.

Tis scoured from the rafter to the bottom cellar stair; And I, —
I leave behind all hope whene'er I enter there;
For the washbrush, like a whirlwind, devastates the peaceful scene,
For Matilda is the cleanest of the cleanest of the clean.

But Matilda's just like Nature, for early every spring
Does Nature get her scrub brush out, her duster and her wing;
With her mighty soap and bucket does she travel all about,
And swashes through the universe and cleans the old thing out.

And she puts up new lace curtains in the windows of the sky,

Made of white cloud mixed with sunshine, floating, filmy tapestry,
When the gorgeous sun at sunset finds the clouds about him curled,
And he sticks his jewelled hairpin through the back hair of the world.

And she takes her dull brown carpet and she rips it from the hills,
And she sprays her floors with showers till they soak through tc the sills ;
Then her tulip-sprinkled carpet, with its background of bright green
Spreads she, rich as is the floor-mat 'neath the high throne of a queen.

So, Matilda, whisk your wash-rag, it is music to my ears,
And it beats in perfect rhythm to the music of the spheres,
Reach your long brush for the cobwebs, swing it ever high and higher,
A baton that beats the measure for the mighty Cosmic Choir.

You are cleaning house with Nature, you are stepping to the march
To which the planet legions trail across the starry arch.
Though the table's on the bureau, and the whisk broom does not cease,
I will eat my supper standing, lapped in universal peace.

THE MAN WHO BRINGS UP THE REAR END.

FOLKS watch the drum major and say "see him come !"
And the fellow who plays on the fife,
And the rub-a-dub man who beats the big drum,
And the bugler who blows for dear life.
They go with the music; they march with the noise;
For the chief in the van they all hunt,
There is smiling of maidens and shouting of boys,
And cheering of men — in the front.
But there's never a cheer that gladdens the ear,
Nor the shout of a brother or friend,
For the mud spattered man who has dropped from the van,
For the man who brings up the rear end.

Not a bravo is heard, not a word, not a word,
As they see him stub on round the bend;
Not a cheer from the churls, not a smile from the girls,
For the man who brings up the rear end !

There are shouts for the victor whose name like a star,
Rose red from the hot clouds of fame,
Thro' the battle smoke of a lurid war,
To climb up the heaven of fame.
And his ears are beset with a tumult of tongues,
That prate of the danger he braved,
With a chorus of praise from the lusty lungs
Of the men of the land he has saved.
But I sing of the man who has dropped from the van,
From the front he could never defend,
Who could never await the harsh volleys of fate —
The man who brings up the rear end !

Then a good strong shout in the rear of the rout,
And the brotherly cheer of a friend;
A cheer that shall start from the core of the heart,
For the man who brings up the rear end.

And who are the men who bring up the rear end?
The laggards too weak to be great ?
Time's water-logged timber too rotten to mend?
Abortions and weaklings of fate?
Not so : There are poets whose songs are unsung,
And singers of wonderful tone,
Reformers whose thunderous words might have stung
To the roots of a tottering throne !
Then shout your huzzas and your loudest hurrahs,
Until the loud welkin shall rend;

Let your loud plaudits grace the world-weary face
Of the man who brings up the rear end !
Then shout without fear for the man in the rear,
Let your heaven-scaling plaudits ascend !
Cry aloud ! cry aloud ! you men there in the crowd !
For the man who brings up the rear end !

There are plebeian souls who sit on a throne,
And Kings who wear never a crown;
There are long-gowned priests who are devils unknown,
And saints in the frock of the clown;
There are hearts that are black 'neath the King's purple vest,
And white 'neath the swain's drilling frock,
And the laborer's coat may be armor the best
For meeting adversity's shock.
Then a cheer and a roar, and three cheers more,
For the man most in need of a friend;
Good cheer for the man who has dropped from the van,
The man who brings up the rear end 1
Then shout your cheer right into his ear,
Let your voices in unity blend;
One loud, long shout in the rear of the rout,
For the man who brings up the rear end !

WHEN THE LEAVES TURN RED.

THERE is a purple peacefulness that covers nature's features,
Like a many-colored bed-quilt o'er a baby's trundle bed,
Nature covers all us children, nervous, tired little creatures,
Nervous, tired little children, whether princes, popes or preachers;
When the leaves turn red.
A balm that's full of sleepiness envelops hill and river,
An air that's full of sweet content o'er all the earth is spread;

We know we dream, and yet we pray to be awakened never,
For 'tis the prayer of every soul to dream right on forever;
When the leaves turn red.

UNCLE SETH ON THE CZAR

WITH a coat uv mail
With an iron tail,
Thet dangles ag'in'
His pants uv tin,
The czar he walks, with a rattlin' roar,
Like a yearthquake through er hardware store.

His boots er zinc
They clank an' clink
With a rattlin' peal,
On his socks er steel;
W'en he sets on his throne, it soun's, by gum,
Like a tin pan fallin' onto a drum.

But then, his shirt
Won't show the dirt,
It's made of iron
Thet's hard to pry on,
With a bosom front of w'ite steel plate,
Thet a dynamite bomb can't penetrate.

An' wide an' far
He rules, the czar;
But I wouldn't swap
My tater crop,
An' the luv of little Tom an' his ma,
Fer the hull wide kingdom uv the czar.

THEN AG'IN—

JIM BOWKER, he said ef he'd had a fair show,
And a big enough town for his talents to grow,
And the least bit assistance in hoein' his row,
Jim Bowker, he said,
He'd filled the world full of the sound of his name,
An' clim the top round in the ladder of fame;
It may have been so;
I dunno;
Jest so it might been,
Then ag'in —

But he had tarnal luck—everythin' went ag'in him,
The arrers er fortune they alius 'ud pin him;
So he didn't get no chance to show off what was in him,
Jim Bowker he said,
Ef he'd had a fair show, you couldn't tell where he'd come,
An' the feats he'd a-done, and the heights he'd a-clumb —
It may have been so;
I dunno;
Jest so it might been,
Then ag'in —

But we're all like Jim Bowker, thinks I, more or less —
Charge fate for our bad luck, ourselves for success,
An' give fortune the blame for all our distress,
As Jim Bowker, he said.
If it hadn' been for luck an' misfortune an' sich,
We might a-been famous, an' might a-been rich,
It might be jest so;
I dunno;

Jest so it might been,
Then ag'in—

THE VOICE.

IN the silence of the desert and the thunder of the shore,
In the lonesome midnight watches, in the market's loud uproar,
Comes the nameless voice whose music soundeth on for-
evermore.
Giving strength to all aweary, giving hope when life is dreary;
Giving fervor to our dullness, giving patience, peace and power.

Tis the song the singer sings not, but the song he hopes to sing;
'Tis the word the prophet brings not, but the word God bade him bring —
But its import is too heavenly for human uttering.
Hence the south wind's sounding motion, and the surf-wash of the ocean,
And the pine's moan on the mountains is its fitting rendering.

NO SHOW.

JOE BEAL 'ud set upon a kaig
Down to the groc'ry store an' throw
One laig right over t'other laig,
An' swear he'd never had no show;
"Oh no," said Joe,
" Hain't hed no show."—
Then shift his quid to t'other jaw,
An' chaw, an' chaw, an' chaw, an' chaw.

He said he got no start in life,
Didn't get no money from his dad,
The washin' took in by his wife

Earned all the funds he ever had;
"Oh no," said Joe,
" Hain't hed no show."—
An' then he'd look up at the clock,
An' talk, an' talk, an' talk, an' talk.

" I've waited twenty year,—le's see—
Yes, twenty-four, an' never struck,
Altho' I've sot roun' patiently,
The fust tarnashion streak er luck.
Oh no," said Joe,
" Hain't hed no show."—
Then stuck like mucilage to the spot,
An' sot, an' sot, an' sot, an' sot.

" I've come down regerler every day
For twenty years to Piper's store;
I've sot here in a patient way,
Say, hain't I, Piper?" Piper swore,
" I tell yer, Joe,
Yer hev no show,
Yer too dern patient,"—ther hull raft
Jest laffed, an' laffed, an' laffed, an' laffed

THE GLABBERGASTIKONIAK.

OLD crazy Kate roams through the hills
Where all the rocks are dumb,
And to the streams and silent woods
Tells of the wrath to come. She cries,
" Each heart shall break with grief
And every soul shall groan,
When the Glabbergastikoniak

Shall come unto his own.

" And then shall laughter turn to tears,
And honey turn to gall,
The blackness of eternal night
Shall then be over all;
And in a starless wilderness
Each soul shall walk alone, W
hen the Glabbergastikoniak
Shall come unto his own.

" Give ear, give ear," cries crazy Kate,
" The time is drawing near
When all the mountains of the world
Shall reel and quake with fear,
And men who rail and scoff and laugh
Shall gnash their teeth and groan,
When the Glabbergastikoniak
Shall come unto his own."

So Kate proclaims the phantom wild
Her jangled brain has reared,
But her Glabbergastikoniak
Has never yet appeared-
But still she waits the coming time,
There in the wilds alone,
When the Glabbergastikoniak
Shall come unto his own.

We rear our phantoms of the mind,
Strange, shadowy shapes of fear,
Our Glabbergastikoniaks
Are ever drawing near.

But every morn the sun breaks forth,
The night's dark mists uproll,
We see no more the forms that vexed
The twilight of the soul.

And men pursuing beckoning fears
O'er phantom moors and fells,
Have pictured awful judgment days
And lurid burning hells;
But as the world wheels into light
This truth is understood:
The universe is always safe,
For God, is always good.
And lapped in the eternal law
There's no such thing as fear,
Our Glabbergastikoniaks
Will never more appear.

Sail forth serene into the dark,
Exultant, fearless, free,
The Glabbergastikoniak
Shall never come to thee.

SWEETS

OH, these rondeaus and triolets are pretty as violets,
They're dainty, artistic and neat; They're Gallic,
Parisian, and pinks of precision,
And veritable sweets for the sweet.
They give a soft pleasure to young men of leisure —
Those beautiful feminine men —
Who on literature's border crochet and embroider,
And do " fancy-work " with the pen.

Their sapless aridities, their dry insipidities,

In statuesque beauty are wrought,
But 'twould be unconventional to express an intentional
Wilful original thought.

NO BEGGARS OR PEDLERS ALLOWED.

NO beggars or pedlers allowed in here !
" If I were a rich man, and king of the mart,
I wouldn't have that phrase on my doorposts appear,
To notify men of my hardness of heart.

If I were a rich man, a beggar would be
That man, of all others, my notice to court;
The one wreck to whom, in my sun-lighted sea,
To throw out my tow-line, and drag into port.

And the pedler, I'd feel he and I were a pair:
For how does a pedler differ from me ? —
From me, with my warehouses towering in air ?
I'm a pedler myself slightly larger than he.

All merchants are pedlers, who barter and strain,
Some with stores for their goods, some with goods on their backs;
All hucksters and hawkers, all crying for gain,
And differing only in size of their packs.

If I were a big pedler, peddling my wares
From a two-acre storehouse, eight stories high,
I wouldn't kick the small pedler over my stairs,
For, perchance, he's as honest a pedler as I.

POEMS BY SPECIALISTS.

JUNE.

BY A FARMER.

THE breachy year has hawed and geed
Through rain, and hail, and snow,
But now plump in a bank of flowers
The driver hollers " whoa ! "

The months, like wild, unruly steers
Have pranced through snow and mud,
But June is like a peaceful cow
Who calmly chews her cud.

She stands there while a deathless grace
Beams from her lustrous eyes,
While round her hum the honey bees,
And flit the butterflies.

Oh, gentlest mooly of the year,
Thy charms too soon shall cease,
Your luscious butter of content,
Your milk of perfect peace!

WINTER.

BY AN ACTOR.

THE snow-flakes filling all the air
Fall slowly all the day,

Like programmes dropped by gallery gods
Down on to the parquet;

The leafless branches cracking loud
Above the tempest's roar
Sound like the beat of countless hands
That call for an encore.

The Storm King down the wintry blast
In mighty paces glides,
In tragic, histrionic steps,
Like Henry Irving's strides;
The snow upon the frozen ground
Is lying deep and thick,
White as an actress' pallid face,
Who eateth arsenic.

SPRING.

BY A PHYSICIAN.

BY bursting buds I diagnose,
And by the birds that sing,
And by the mild balsamic air,
The symptoms of the Spring.
The clouds, like generous allopaths,
Pour down their drastic doses
To swell the germs of bud and spray
And the incipient roses.

Winter, that ailment of the year,
With care I think will leave her,
But oft returns again, much like

An intermittent fever.
With sun baths and with shower baths
Let the frail Spring resist him
Till she has time to expurgate
The ailment from her system.

NEW YEAR'S.
BY A PRINTER.
THE years pass on in rapid flight —
Time neither sleeps nor nods;
They come like frequent paragraphs,
All interspersed with quads.
The days drop in like well-filled lines,
The nights like "leads" are thick,
Old time is standing at his " case."
And filling up his " stick."

And now he takes another " take,"
A copy all unread,
Which fate, like a stern editor,
Before his gaze has spread.
So, let the years pass on and on,
Through sunshine and through storms,
Until the foreman calls the hour
For " locking up the forms."

COMING OF WINTER.

BY A CARPENTER.

THE dead leaves rustle from the bough
Like shavings from a plank;
Each tree stands mortised in the ground,

And lifts its moveless shank;
Each limb, a rafter cold and bare,
The heartless blast receives, —
No clapboards of fair fruits and flowers,
No shingles of green leaves.

The mallets of the driving sleet
Descend with sturdy blows,
And thro' the rafters of the sky
Like sawdust fall the snows;
The woodchuck in his chiseled hole
In torpid sleep is curled;
The storm king with his mighty skid
Is shaking up the world.

AN EARLY FROST.

BY A BARBER.

THE grass, like whiskers on the earth,
Was waving fair and free;
The tufted moss grew on the rocks
Much like a French goatee;
The garden smiled beneath mine eye
Thro' all the livelong hours,
And lifted toward the summer sky
It's sweet moustache of flowers.

But ah ! the cruel frost came down
Where those sweet flowerets grew,
And lathered all the landscape o'er
With its cold, white shampoo !
So Time's keen razor shaves us all;

By our wild prayers unvexed
He stands and hones his gleaming edge,
And sternly murmurs " Next" !

WINTER.

BY A MASON.

THE ice has plastered o'er the lake
With plastering smooth and thick,
The hoar frost sticks upon the grass
Like mortar on a brick.
Up the steep ladder of the year
Does toiling winter go,
And bends beneath his heavy load,
His hod of ice and snow.

With smoothing trowel in his hand
He makes the snow walls shine,
And the white polished lakelet's breast
He'll quickly kalsomine.
With bricks of hail and hair of sleet
His masonry is wrought,
And down the storm blast's echoing path
He yells, " More mort, more mort! "

WINTER.

BY A LAWYER.

A HEARTLESS lien upon the year
Is held by winter hoar,
A mortgage and a heartless lien

As told hereinbefore.
Bright summer now is dispossessed,
No more her face entrances,
Gone with her chattels and effects,
And her appurtenances.

Yes, summer gives a quit-claim deed
Of all her rosy dower,
A well-attested bill of sale
Of fountain, fruit and flower —
Of all her earthly goods, to wit:
Buds, leaves, streams, held by her,
And winter is appointed heir
And sole executor.

THINGS THAT DIDN'T OCCUR.

I'VE come to the conclusion that there ain't nothin' true,
An' nothin' tells such monstrous lies as school-books uster do.
Columbus found this country out, the school-books uster state;
But now they say he landed here four hundred years too late.
A chap named Ericson deserves the fame of the event,
An' poor Columbus' voyages were much too subsequent;
An' so I say the very things that make the greatest stir,
An' the most interestin' things, are things that didn't occur.

An' now they say that Cap'n Kidd tried hard to live upright,
An' that he had no pirate gold he uster hide at night.
But my old school-books uster say he roamed the Spanish main,
An' murdered crews, an' stole their gold, an' then sailed home again.
But now they say he lived upright by honor's rigid rule,
An' good enough to run a bank or lead a Sunday school.
An' so I say the very things that make the greatest stir,

An' the most interestin' things, are things that didn't occur.

A chap named Shakespeare writ so much, long pomes an' plays an' verses,
The school-books said he'd fame enough to fill two universes;
They said his writings were way up, away beyond compare,—
I kinder galloped through 'em once an' thought 'em purty fair ; —
An' now they say he didn't write because he had no brains,
An' say he hardly knew enough to come in when it rains.
An' so I say the very things that make the greatest stir,
An' the most interestin' things, are things that didn't occur.

AN ECONOMICAL MAN.

HE lived on thirteen cents a day, —
Ten cents for milk and cracker,
One cent for dissipation gay,
And two cents for tobacco;
And if he wished an extra dish
He'd take his pole and catch a fish.

And if his stomach raised a war
'Gainst this penurious habit,
He'd go and kill a woodchuck, or
Assassinate a rabbit;
And thus he'd live in sweet content
On food that never cost a cent.

And, that he might lay by in bank
The proceeds of his labor,
He'd happen round at meals, the crank !
And dine upon his neighbor!
And then he'd eat enough to last
Until another day had passed.

He bought nor pantaloons nor vest,
Nor rich, expensive jacket;
He had one suit — his pa's bequest —
He thought would " stand the racket."
He patched it thirty years, 'tis true,
And then declared 'twas good as new.

He owned but one suit to his back,
And minus cuffs and collars.
He died, and left his nephew Jack
Nine hundred thousand dollars !
And Jack he run this fortune through
And only took a year or two.

SHAKESPEARE'S GHOST TO IGNATIUS DONNELLY.

DOW, here comes one Ignatius Donnelly
Hath writ a book wherein he proves, good faith
I writ me not the plays which bear my name
And make such noise and romage through the world.
Marry ! good sir, in faith thou hast embarked
Upon an enterprise with stomach in 't.

Now, prithee, boy, lend me awhile thine ear:
Perchance, so poor a man as Shakespeare is,
Herding with fellows of the baser sort; —
With Homer, Aristophanes, and all
Th' ignoble motley of the muses' train,
The jigging poets of Apollo's rout,
May yet find favor in thy baleful eyes.

Alack ! good sir, you paint me forth a clown,

A vulgar fellow, an unlettered swain,
A usurer, extortioner, and rake —
The multiplying villainies of Nature
Mantle my record like a standing pool!
By cock and pye, sir, you protest too much !

The fleshy vessel which held Shakespeare in
Mayhap was made of crude and earthy stuff;
And you say right, Ignatius, writ no plays,
And heard no music of the choiring spheres.
But, know, this playwright had a wanton fay
Who told him tales of most exalted heaven
And of the lowest deep. Aye, there's the rub !
He made Will Shakespeare, coarse, unlettered hind,
Wise with a wisdom that ye wot not of.

This fay, this Puck, this nimble Ariel,
Told tales that Francis Bacon never heard.
Go to ! Ignatius, get thee to thy rest.
Pillow the temples of thy ciphering head
On the black waters of oblivion.
But Shakespeare's plays, good sir, some several years
Shall yet be read, methinks, by divers men.

HOT WEATHER PHILOSOPHY.

LET us sail on our way, free from sorrow's embargo,
As content with ourselves as a man from Chicago.
Let us feel our best day, the one freest from sorrow,
Is the day after yesterday, just 'fore to-morrow.
Though 'tis hot enough here let us think how much drearier
Is the 'glomerate mass of earth's molten interior;
Though 'tis hot enough here, let us cool our red faces

By the thought of the cold in the interstellar spaces;
Though we're lurid and red as a furnace-burnt ember,
Let us think of the snow-drifts and ice of December;
Though Sol in his fervor grows stronger and stronger
Yet the sun will freeze up in ten million years longer;
Though the sun through the heavens rides his fiery bicycle
In a few million years he'll be cold as an icicle.
So let us rejoice at the grand consummation,
And grow happy and frigid in anticipation.

LINES.

Read at the Beta Theta Pi National Convention, at Wooglin-on-Chautauqua,
the evening of August 4,1899.

JUST why this event should be reckoned completer
With a solemn old bard to address you in metre,
And why he should read you a metrical lecture,
This solemn old bard has no means of conjecture.
But since it so happens the good boys of Beta
Are thirsting for verse and are wilting for metre,
And are lonesome and lorn as a man who is single,
Till their bachelor prose has been married to jingle,
My mill has ground out, with its old imperfections,
Some sober and somnolent-solemn reflections.

As swift years go by and life's ripe apple mellows,
Our memory reverts to young days with " the fellows,"
When we, with the ladder supplied by the college,
Tried to climb the top limb of the old tree of knowledge.
When we dug, as the farmer will dig the potato,
For the tuber of thought in the rich soil of Plato;
When we strolled 'neath the sunrise, and each a glad roamer

Through the dewy demesne of that morning bard, Homer;
Took one gill of Homer (and raised no loud clamor)
Diluted with infinite gallons of grammar.
 • And the thought will arise, and it's often repeated,
In that classical dram we were wofully cheated.
There were many deep bards and fine poets, they tell us,
And sages revered in that old land of Hellas,
But we felt not the spell of their deep necromancy,
The charm of their wisdom, or the fire of their fancy,

For all we could do was to stand up and stammer
Some formula-phrases of pitiful grammar.
While we ate the peel of our syntax potato
We missed all the soul and the genius of Plato;
While we fed upon crusts, like a tramp and a roamer,
We missed the white bread in the pantries of Homer.

There were thinkers who lived by the sunlit Egean,
Who soared through the blue of thought's high empyrean;
And we, like bold fledglings, were eager to follow —
For the gray mountain eagle is chased by the swallow —
But we never could chase these aerial whizzers
For our wings were all clipped by grammatical scissors.
Then let every Beta lad take his small hammer
And smite, without pity, this monster of grammar.
Let us get at the pith of the marrow of the ages;
Let us get at the core of the soul of the sages;
Let us find the world's heart in its central pulsations;
Let us search for the thought that has moulded the nations;
Let us seek for the spirit, strong, vital and pure,
That lives in the heart of all true literature;
Let us seek men to teach us its grace and its glamour,
And shun the prim, pitiful peddlers of grammar.

But, in spite of the heavy, light-darkening blinders,
Swathed over our eyes by the dull gerund-grinders;
In spite of the roots of the higher mathematics —
When we wished we were girls and could cry at quadratics,—
We revert to those times when young hope swelled our bellows,
And our hearts beat with joy as we think of the fellows !

The fellows of Beta — our life seems completer
When we think of those days and the fellows of Beta.
And now, when we do anything that is clever,
And deem that we stand on the heights of endeavor,
We feel that mankind should announce it and show it,
And, foremost of all, let the Beta boys know it.
When we're made selectman or a highway surveyor,
Are elected town clerk, or are mentioned for mayor,
When we've published a pamphlet, or written a ditty,
Or served for three years on the high school committee,
Let the trumpets of fame o'er the wide planet blow it —
But, foremost of all, let the Beta boys know it.

But when we are weak and our life seems a failure,
And the world is a desert from here to Australia;
When we're sentenced to jail for some crime of foul nature,
Or are members elect of our state legislature —
Let the big world at large all derisively jeer of it,
But, for love of your life, let no Beta boy hear of it!

Those were days when no fetters of fortune confined us,
When we gazed on the infinite ocean behind us,
And gazed on the mist-bannered mountains before us,
While Hope, o'er their summits triumphantly bore us.
Fate said, " Rule the earth and dethrone the usurpers,"

And each of us answered, " I'm here for that purpose."
Our consciousness told us the crazy old planet
Was wobbly and wild, needing some one to man it,
Some wise ruling genius to guide it and veer it,
Some strong, pilot hand to direct it and steer it,
Some imperial genius to keep the thing steady—
And each of us answered, " I'm ready ! I'm ready! "

True, when we were loaded for bear or for bison,
We banged at the stars or shot at the horizon,
So the bison and bear by our guns were ungingered,
And the stars and horizon are thus far uninjured,
And the high heavens are still by our bullets unblighted,
And the rivers of earth still flow on unignited.

But, if we've not struck the high target we aimed at,
Tis nothing we need to regret and be 'shamed at
Right here, to give zest to this metrical salad
And point a good moral, is given this ballad,
A fact, and not a mere fanciful caper,
And I know it is true, for I read it i' the paper —

Says the cabin boy to Sambo, the cook, —
And a tear fell round and great, —
" I won't bear the yoke of every ol' poke,
An' take off my cap to the mate.
For I've a notion the Indian Ocean — "
And he stood up proud and free,
" Has no cabin boy than is better than Oi —
Let him take off his hat to me ! "

" Hole on, dar, chile," says Sambo, the cook,
" An' lean yer yere to me,

You ain't no boss clar way ercross
This yere hull big blame sea.
Hain't yer seen it happ'n how the mate to the cap'n
Takes off his hat? Go long !
You's awful brash, you young w'ite trash,
Jes' larn ware you belong ! "

' Belay there, Sambo ! " says the boy to the cook,
" Don't get ez hot ez a stove,
Did you ever see it happ'n thet our ol' cap'n
Tips his hat to any cove ? "
" W'y, now you're wrong," says Sambo. " Go 'long!
Jump overboard an' swim, For he'd be a Jonah if he didn' smoove de owner
An tip his hat to him ! "

" Avast there, Sambo," says the boy to the cook,
"Your sails is too much spread,
The owner's a stunner, a twenty thousan' tonner,
An' he keeps his hat on his head ! "
" Break off dar, chile ! break off foh erwhile !
Here de merchant jines de swim,
An' dat's wot's de marter w'en he wants his charter,
Den de cap'n tips to him !"

" But the merchant," says the boy, " is a god-on-wheels,
A reg'lar tough ol' duff! "
" Laws ! " Sambo said, " let me fill yo' head
Wiv some kine er sense an' stuff!
De merchant's a seller, a trad'n feller,
An' he wants to sell, yer see !
So he ben' down flat, an' he take off he hat,
An' he bow to you an' me ! "

Haec fabula docet: this poor fable teaches,
We're all in one basket, the same kind of peaches.
In the cabin, on deck, where our station may happen,
To some man, or some men, we are each of us cap'n.
And we sail the same sea to a port far before us,
With the same pilot stars shining placidly o'er us;
And meet the same waves, the same tempest's resistance,
And make for a harbor that's far in the distance.

A GLANCE BEHIND AND AHEAD.

[Read at the decennial supper of the class of 1882, Brown University, June 21,1892.]

THIS year the corridors of Fame re-echo through and through
With Christopher Columbus and the class of '82.
Four hundred years ago he sailed to seek a world, and thus
Ten years ago we woke to find a world a-seeking us.
And for the world we have no thought but one of deep regret,
If it has bungled in its search and hasn't found us yet.
We feel the dull world doesn't know (that lets us still be hid)
A good thing when it sees it, same as old Columbus did.
Ten years ago we slipped the tight, scholastic collar free —
But the river, unignited, still flows onward to the sea.
Then we thought that fate would meet us with a special hullaballoo
With her hand outstretched to greet us, — " Glad to see ye ! Howdy do?"
And we thought we saw the promise of great empires in her eye,
And she seeking kings to rule them, and each answered, " Here am I."

Though we knew the great earth wobbled on its axis as it whirled,
Still we thought 'twas no great matter — we could reconstruct the world.
(But I'll say in a parenthesis — reporters please omit —
Though we have begun the business we have not quite finished yet.)

Though I hate to make admissions that detract from our just fame,
Still, I must allow, the planet seems to wobble just the same.
Though we have not clasped the Vision that once crowned the morning hill
In the early forenoon sunshine, we will chase the Vision still.
Though she fades into the distance of the hazy amethyst,
Though she's aureoled with rainbows and her garments are of mist,

Still she beckons — we are coming! See her right hand pointing high
Toward her misty mountains yonder, where her mighty empires lie.
And we follow through the noontide till the closing of the day,
See, she beckons — We are coming — We are coming. Lead the way.

TWO SONGS.

THE spirit that sings in the moaning pine,
And has sung since the world began,
Is gloomy as night when the stars do not shine,
And sad as the heart of man.
The spirit that sings in the laughing brook,
And has sung since the world began,
Is gay as the joy of a maiden's look,
And glad as the heart of man.

I lay 'neath the pine, on the brink of the brook,
And their two songs rose in the air;
One, sweet as the laugh from an Oread's nook,
One, heavy with sobs of despair.

And the sad and the glad mingled into one strain,
But made no dissonant strife,
As the varying tones of pleasure and pain
Mingle into the music of life.

And I said: " Lo ! the song of the heart of man,
The song of gloom and of glee,
The song that has been since the world began,
The song that ever shall be."

TWO PRAYERS.

OUR minister gets up to pray and lets the spirit flow,
An' tells the Lord a lot er things he thinks He ought to know,
Tells Him about the gover'ment, how politics 'ill turn—
Coz He don't mix in politics an' hez no way to learn.

He preaches on the Presidunt an' describes his evil natur',
An' gives away the Cabinet an' our venal legislator',
Shows how corruption festers, an' tells of things, I fear,
Thet the Lord—they come so sudden—will be surprised to hear.

He takes the cyclopedy an' he weaves it in his prayer,
Sandwiched in with choice statistics which he picks up every-where ;
They say the Lord knows everything,— sometimes
I uster doubt,
Now I know—our pastor tells him — thet's the way he fin's it out.

In the meetin' t'other evenin' he lifted up his face
An' much interestin' gossip laid before the Throne of Grace,
Chunks of useful information did he shrewdly intersperse,
Thet would make the Lord enlightened ez to all the universe.

Then Jim Drew, the drunken sailor, jest riz up there in the aisle,
An' though 'twas in a holy place we couldn't forbear to smile.
But Deacon Briggs he nudged me hard; sez he, " Don't grin thet way,
For don't ye see he's sober, an' the rascal's goin' to pray."

He started in an' sez, " O Lord ! I'm jest chuckful er sin,
An' there ain't no place, I reckin, for yer mercy to squeeze in,
For I'm jist good for nothin', an' an ol' wreck from the sea;
Take me—I ain't wuth takin'—but I give myself to Thee."

Then he broke down an' blubbered out, an' jest set down to bawl,
An' then there came a loud " Amen " thet near bust through the wall;
We knew a spark of heavenly fire hed touched this earthly clod,
For his soul in all its nakedness had shown itself to God.

There warn't much learnin' in his prayer, but yet it travelled far,
An' went floatin' up to glory where the shinin' angels are;
The pastor's prayer so weighted down 'ith Aggers, facts and proof,
Got lodged among the rafters an' didn't get beyond the roof.

THE BABY KING OF SPAIN.

A MURDEROUS plot, of late laid bar
Has shocked all nations everywhere
A plot hatched in a madman's brair
To kill the baby king of Spain.
The strong old Roman hates still cling
Around the very name of King;
And good men hope to see laid prone
The height of every towering throne.
Smite kingcraft strong between the eyes;
And when the death-struck monster dies
A cry of joy our hearts will give—
But let the little baby live.

A baby—king by right divine,
A monarch of an ancient line,

The mightiest in this world of ours
Of principalities and powers.
No conquering captain ever known
This sturdy king can disenthrone;
His throne defended from all darts
Is borne upon his subject's hearts.
The whirlwinds of all wars that blow
This throne can never overthrow.
His royal right all men confess,
His sovereign strength of helplessness;
And 'tis an infinite coward's arm
Upraised to do a baby harm.
Kill kingcraft; it deserves to die;
But pass the royal baby by !

Bad, wicked kings have ruled in Spain,
And wicked kings may rule again.
Kill kingcraft, but protect the king—
That laughing, babbling, helpless thing.
Kill kingcraft, for his many years
Are dark with stains of blood and tears.
And even now with laboring breath,
He stumbles, tottering, near to death ;
And, for his crimes in days gone by
The grey old wretch deserves to die;
God to the hand new strength impart,
That drives the dagger through his heart,
And buries from the light of day
This lingering incubus away.
Kill kingcraft; all men will forgive;
Kill him; but let the baby live.

WHEN SHAKESPEARE SLINGS HIMSELF.

I TRIED to read w'at Shakespeare writ
An' never thought no great of it.
I knew no man in our town
Skurce ekilled Shakespeare in renown,
But still, I reckoned all the time
He warn't ez smart ez ol' Squire Prime.
Though others stuck him on a pole,
I alius laid him on the shelf,
Because he had no spurt an' soul,
An' never slung himself.

An' ev'ry time I tried I'd fail
To make out either head or tail,
Or any heart, or sense, or soul
To all his wobblin* rigmarole.
No matter how he'd squirm an' try
He couldn't come up to ol' Bill Nye.
An' so I'd shet the book again,
An' stick it up there on the shelf,
An' say " It's plain to me, it's plain
Thet he couldn't sling himself."

An elocutioner come down
One night, last fall, to our town,
An' advertised fer sev'rul days
Thet he would read from Shakespeare's plays.
"The feller," sez I, "is a chump
To try to read from such a gump.
If I couldn't write ez well ez him
I'd lay myself upon the shelf;

Fer Shakespeare hain't no swing and vim,
An' he can't sling himself."
I heered the elocutioner spout,
An' he just turned me wrong side out.
Them words — like cannon balls they hit —
Them words thet William Shakespeare writ.
An' each word struck a tender part
An' landed red-hot in my heart.
W'y, I clum up life's highest stair
An' et from Natur's tip top shelf
An' heered thet reader r'ar an' tear
An' Shakespeare sling himself!

W'y Shakespeare took the heart er man
An' coined it into words, I swan.
An' every word he coined is still
Worth more'n a twenty dollar bill.
An' some words gambol, like young steers,
An' some are drippin' wet 'ith tears;
For Shakespeare et the sweetest meat
On Mother Nature's highest shelf,
An' ev'ry day he went to eat
An' then he slung himself!

W'y here's a man who waded through
The drippin' daisies an' the dew,
An' who in highest heaven did dwell,
An' wandered through the lowest hell.
An' he communion uster hoi'
With God an' devil in the soul,

Who searched his soul in every part,
An' ransacked every nook an' shelf,

Who looked right in his open heart,
An' went an' slung himself.

W'en Shakespeare slings himself I see
How big a human soul can be,
I feel like claimin' as my own
The highest seat aroun' the throne.
W'en Shakespeare slung himself, I say,
W'at angel could do better, hey?
An' so we know we hev the best,
The sweetest from the highest shelf,
The brightest, grandest, purtiest,
When Shakespeare slings himself!

THE READY-MADE MAN.

SOME sages of Hindustan,
Of eruditical lore,
Determined to make a ready-made man,
Which had never been done before;
All this, you know,
Was some time ago,
In the pre-historical yore.

So they mixed their chemicals up
In a mighty porcelain bowl,
And they stirred them up as you'd stir up a cup
Of coffee or tea, on my soul;
Made a hole in the batter,
And set on a platter,
With carbon and salt in the hole.

These sages of Hindustan

Then poured the chemicals in;
Their phosphoric acid they poured from a pan,
And their soda and gelatine,
With butyric acid,
To make the flesh flaccid,
And water and creatine.

And they made the form of a man,
Organically sound and complete,
And they found, these sages of Hindustan,
No flaw from his head to his feet;
And one of their fellows
Blew air from a bellows,
And the man leaped up from his seat.

They'd made the ready made man,
But he was crazy and wild,
He howled like a beast in a caravan,
And then he cried like a child;
They put magnesia on
His left brain ganglion
To make him reconciled.

And this—it made him hum—
Twas withering flame to fuel
And they took chloride of potassium
And mixed it in his gruel;
Then he acted like a fool
Who had never been to school —
His idiot groans were cruel.

Then carbon from the pan,
They placed beneath his crown:

Then he fought like John L. Sullivan,
And knocked the sages down.
Then the sages of Hindustan
They killed the ready-made man
Who had done them up so brown.

My moral all may scan,
For it's designed to show
That the making of a perfect man
Is a process rather slow;
The perfect fellow
Needs time to mellow,
And plenty of time to grow.

WALT WHITMAN.

BONE has the savor from the salt
With Walt.
An untamed stallion, strong and sure,
He galloped through our literature;
No critic trainer had the grit
To tame him to the bridle bit,
No rein his headlong speed could halt,
Unharnessed Walt.

A man of many a flaw and fault
Was Walt.
He never tried to train his thought
To blossom in a flower pot;
With careless hand he flung his seeds,
And some grew roses, some grew weeds,
And some rich flowers of purple blood
Sprung from the mud.

O'er custom's fence, with easy vault,
Leaped Walt.
The pedant's gown he would not don,
Nor hold his pen with handcuffs on.
His rhythm, like a fetterless sea,
Broke in mad music and debris
Against the bowlders of his age
With giant rage.

We shall not find 'neath heaven's vault
Another Walt.
He gave a gift beyond all pelf
Man's greatest gift — he gave himself.
Then bear, with dead hands on his breast,
This shaggy old man to his rest.
A strong audacious soul has fled,
Now Walt is dead.

A TRAGIC END.

HE worked for eight dollars a week,
So his prodigal wants were repressed;
But he had an imposing physique,
Which he longed to keep perfectly dressed —
A superb and commanding physique,
He was bound to keep thoroughly dressed.

But his suit, it was never complete;
If he had an immaculate hat,
And the daintiest shoes on his feet,
He would have a dejected cravat;
Wear twelve-dollar shoes on his feet

And a picayune style of cravat.

If he bought a cravat that was new,
Then his shoes would be out at the toes ;
Let him struggle the best he could do,
He'd wear some undesirable clo'es —
Let him torture the best he could do,
He'd have some unconventional clo'es.

If his beaver was shiny and sleek,
And his coat and his ulster ***au fait*** —
Yet he worked for eight dollars a week,
And his trousers were rusty and gray —
He toiled for eight dollars a week;
Hence his trousers were baggy and gray.

But at last his whole suit was complete,
And he walked forth in glory and pride,
Well-dressed from his head to his feet;
But that very same hour he died —
Well-dressed from his head to his feet —
In the hour of triumph he died.

THL GRASSVALE RAILROAD.

GRASSVALE lay hidden in the hills in indolent repose —
It lay there like a snowflake in the bosom of a rose —
Against the mountains on the East the East winds vainly pressed,
And the mountains stopped the fury of the storm-burst from the West.

But the Grassvale people waited for a railroad to come down
And tunnel through the mountains and wind grandly into town;
Through the weed-grown streets of Grassvale men would saunter to and fro,

And tell how, when the railroad came, the little town would grow.

Every night to Durkee's grocery came a crowd of men to talk it,
With big empires in their fancy and two nickels in their pocket;
But the cows trod down the dahlias in each housewife's small front yard,
And whole droves of pigs went rooting down the village boulevard.

Every morn the magic sunrise all the Eastern hills would streak,
And God fling his sunset banner from the topmost Western peak,
But moss grew on the houses where no paint had yet appeared,
As the face that has no beauty is the first to raise a beard.

The chimney of the old town hall was thrown down by the rain,
And they stuck a rusty funnel through the bottom window pane;
At the Baptist church the steeple blew off one tempestuous day,
And they left it as a rendezvous where hens could go and lay.

The great dream of the railroad banished their uneasy fears,
Although they had a suit of clothes but once in thirteen years;
For they reasoned when the railroad should come winding down their way
They would have a pair of trousers almost every other day.

And we all wait for our railroad, while our front yards grow with thistle,
Lie and listen in our valley for the locomotive's whistle;
Yes, we build up mighty railroads in our superheated brain,
While we ought to climb our mountains and just foot it to the train.

THE COSMIC POEM.

ALL motion is rhythm, says wise Herbert Spencer,
A sage so immense that no sage is immenser.
All the worlds wobble on with a rhythmical teeter,
And the universe whirls on its mystical metre.

The sage sees the stars, and their rhythmic orbs show him
That the world is a verse and the Cosmos a poem.

The torn sea that surges with wreck-scattered trophies
Beats out its great theme in tumultuous strophes;
The blind winds that blow from the caverns of chaos,
Or the zephyrs of twilight that soothe and allay us,
The rivers that leap from the high precipices
Whose foam-banners wave o'er the startled abysses,
Or the gay brook that makes the long lilies grow sweeter —
All these, one and all, are a part of the metre.

And all lives are a poem; some wild and cyclonic
With verses of cynical bluster Byronic;
And some still flow on in perpetual benison,
As perfect and smooth as a stanza of Tennyson;
And some find huge boulders their currents to hinder
And are broken and bent like the poems of Pindar;
And some a deep base of proud music are built on —
The calm ocean swell of the epic of Milton;
And some rollick on with a freedom completer

Bat most lives are mixed like Shakespearian dramas,
Where the king speaks heroics, the idiot stammers,
Where the old man gives counsel, the young man loves hotly,
Where the king wears his crown and the fool wears his motley,
Where the lord treads his hall and the peasant his heather—
And in the fifth act they all exit together, —
And the drama goes out with its pomp and its thunder,
And we weep, and we laugh, and we listen, and wonder!

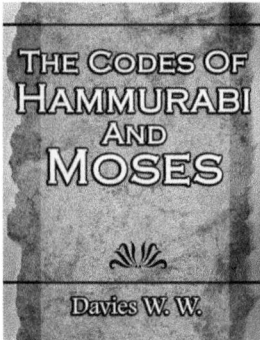

The Codes Of Hammurabi And Moses
W. W. Davies

QTY

The discovery of the Hammurabi Code is one of the greatest achievements of archaeology, and is of paramount interest, not only to the student of the Bible, but also to all those interested in ancient history...

Religion   ISBN: *1-59462-338-4*

Pages:132

MSRP $12.95

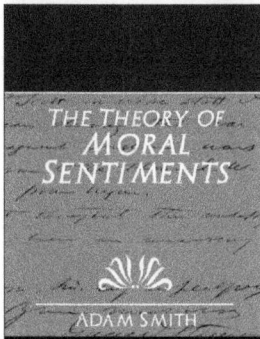

The Theory of Moral Sentiments
Adam Smith

QTY

This work from 1749. contains original theories of conscience amd moral judgment and it is the foundation for systemof morals.

Philosophy ISBN: *1-59462-777-0*

Pages:536

MSRP $19.95

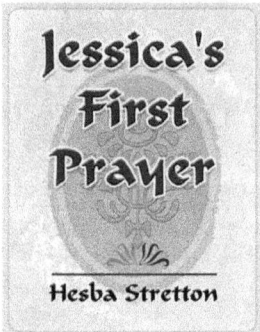

Jessica's First Prayer
Hesba Stretton

QTY

In a screened and secluded corner of one of the many railway-bridges which span the streets of London there could be seen a few years ago, from five o'clock every morning until half past eight, a tidily set-out coffee-stall, consisting of a trestle and board, upon which stood two large tin cans, with a small fire of charcoal burning under each so as to keep the coffee boiling during the early hours of the morning when the work-people were thronging into the city on their way to their daily toil...

Pages:84

Childrens   ISBN: *1-59462-373-2*

MSRP $9.95

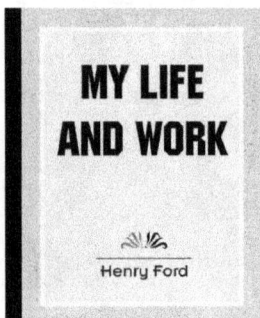

My Life and Work
Henry Ford

QTY

Henry Ford revolutionized the world with his implementation of mass production for the Model T automobile. Gain valuable business insight into his life and work with his own auto-biography... "We have only started on our development of our country we have not as yet, with all our talk of wonderful progress, done more than scratch the surface. The progress has been wonderful enough but..."

Pages:300

Biographies/   ISBN: *1-59462-198-5*

MSRP $21.95

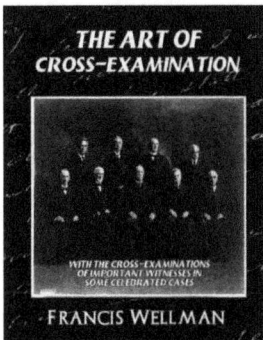

The Art of Cross-Examination
Francis Wellman

QTY

I presume it is the experience of every author, after his first book is published upon an important subject, to be almost overwhelmed with a wealth of ideas and illustrations which could readily have been included in his book, and which to his own mind, at least, seem to make a second edition inevitable. Such certainly was the case with me; and when the first edition had reached its sixth impression in five months, I rejoiced to learn that it seemed to my publishers that the book had met with a sufficiently favorable reception to justify a second and considerably enlarged edition. ..

Reference   ISBN: *1-59462-647-2*

Pages:412
MSRP $19.95

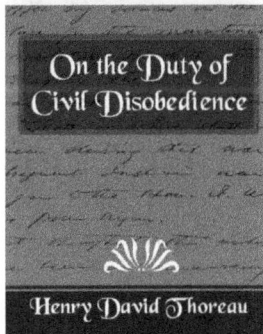

On the Duty of Civil Disobedience
Henry David Thoreau

QTY

Thoreau wrote his famous essay, On the Duty of Civil Disobedience, as a protest against an unjust but popular war and the immoral but popular institution of slave-owning. He did more than write—he declined to pay his taxes, and was hauled off to gaol in consequence. Who can say how much this refusal of his hastened the end of the war and of slavery ?

Law   ISBN: *1-59462-747-9*

Pages:48
MSRP $7.45

Dream Psychology Psychoanalysis for Beginners
Sigmund Freud

QTY

Sigmund Freud, born Sigismund Schlomo Freud (May 6, 1856 - September 23, 1939), was a Jewish-Austrian neurologist and psychiatrist who co-founded the psychoanalytic school of psychology. Freud is best known for his theories of the unconscious mind, especially involving the mechanism of repression; his redefinition of sexual desire as mobile and directed towards a wide variety of objects; and his therapeutic techniques, especially his understanding of transference in the therapeutic relationship and the presumed value of dreams as sources of insight into unconscious desires.

Psychology   ISBN: *1-59462-905-6*

Pages:196
MSRP $15.45

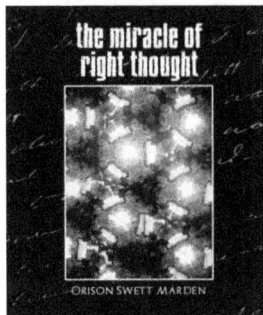

The Miracle of Right Thought
Orison Swett Marden

QTY

Believe with all of your heart that you will do what you were made to do. When the mind has once formed the habit of holding cheerful, happy, prosperous pictures, it will not be easy to form the opposite habit. It does not matter how improbable or how far away this realization may see, or how dark the prospects may be, if we visualize them as best we can, as vividly as possible, hold tenaciously to them and vigorously struggle to attain them, they will gradually become actualized, realized in the life. But a desire, a longing without endeavor, a yearning abandoned or held indifferently will vanish without realization.

Self Help   ISBN: *1-59462-644-8*

Pages:360
MSRP $25.45

www.bookjungle.com *email: sales@bookjungle.com fax: 630-214-0564 mail: Book Jungle PO Box 2226 Champaign, IL 61825*

QTY

The Rosicrucian Cosmo-Conception Mystic Christianity *by Max Heindel*   ISBN: *1-59462-188-8* **$38.95**
The Rosicrucian Cosmo-conception is not dogmatic, neither does it appeal to any other authority than the reason of the student. It is: not controversial, but is: sent forth in the, hope that it may help to clear...
New Age/Religion Pages 646

Abandonment To Divine Providence *by Jean-Pierre de Caussade*   ISBN: *1-59462-228-0* **$25.95**
"The Rev. Jean Pierre de Caussade was one of the most remarkable spiritual writers of the Society of Jesus in France in the 18th Century. His death took place at Toulouse in 1751. His works have gone through many editions and have been republished...
Inspirational/Religion Pages 400

Mental Chemistry *by Charles Haanel*   ISBN: *1-59462-192-6* **$23.95**
Mental Chemistry allows the change of material conditions by combining and appropriately utilizing the power of the mind. Much like applied chemistry creates something new and unique out of careful combinations of chemicals the mastery of mental chemistry...
New Age Pages 354

The Letters of Robert Browning and Elizabeth Barret Barrett 1845-1846 vol II   ISBN: *1-59462-193-4* **$35.95**
by Robert Browning and Elizabeth Barrett
Biographies Pages 596

Gleanings In Genesis (volume I) *by Arthur W. Pink*   ISBN: *1-59462-130-6* **$27.45**
Appropriately has Genesis been termed "the seed plot of the Bible" for in it we have, in germ form, almost all of the great doctrines which are afterwards fully developed in the books of Scripture which follow...
Religion/Inspirational Pages 420

The Master Key *by L. W. de Laurence*   ISBN: *1-59462-001-6* **$30.95**
In no branch of human knowledge has there been a more lively increase of the spirit of research during the past few years than in the study of Psychology, Concentration and Mental Discipline. The requests for authentic lessons in Thought Control, Mental Discipline and...
New Age/Business Pages 422

The Lesser Key Of Solomon Goetia *by L. W. de Laurence*   ISBN: *1-59462-092-X* **$9.95**
This translation of the first book of the "Lemegton" which is now for the first time made accessible to students of Talismanic Magic was done, after careful collation and edition, from numerous Ancient Manuscripts in Hebrew, Latin, and French...
New Age/Occult Pages 92

Rubaiyat Of Omar Khayyam *by Edward Fitzgerald*   ISBN: *1-59462-332-5* **$13.95**
Edward Fitzgerald, whom the world has already learned, in spite of his own efforts to remain within the shadow of anonymity, to look upon as one of the rarest poets of the century, was born at Bredfield, in Suffolk, on the 31st of March, 1809. He was the third son of John Purcell...
Music Pages 172

Ancient Law *by Henry Maine*   ISBN: *1-59462-128-4* **$29.95**
The chief object of the following pages is to indicate some of the earliest ideas of mankind, as they are reflected in Ancient Law, and to point out the relation of those ideas to modern thought.
Religion/History Pages 452

Far-Away Stories *by William J. Locke*   ISBN: *1-59462-129-2* **$19.45**
"Good wine needs no bush, but a collection of mixed vintages does. And this book is just such a collection. Some of the stories I do not want to remain buried for ever in the museum files of dead magazine-numbers an author's not unpardonable vanity..."
Fiction Pages 272

Life of David Crockett *by David Crockett*   ISBN: *1-59462-250-7* **$27.45**
"Colonel David Crockett was one of the most remarkable men of the times in which he lived. Born in humble life, but gifted with a strong will, an indomitable courage, and unremitting perseverance...
Biographies/New Age Pages 424

Lip-Reading *by Edward Nitchie*   ISBN: *1-59462-206-X* **$25.95**
Edward B. Nitchie, founder of the New York School for the Hard of Hearing, now the Nitchie School of Lip-Reading, Inc, wrote "LIP-READING Principles and Practice". The development and perfecting of this meritorious work on lip-reading was an undertaking...
How-to Pages 400

A Handbook of Suggestive Therapeutics, Applied Hypnotism, Psychic Science   ISBN: *1-59462-214-0* **$24.95**
by Henry Munro
Health/New Age/Health/Self-help Pages 376

A Doll's House: and Two Other Plays *by Henrik Ibsen*   ISBN: *1-59462-112-8* **$19.95**
Henrik Ibsen created this classic when in revolutionary 1848 Rome. Introducing some striking concepts in playwriting for the realist genre, this play has been studied the world over.
Fiction/Classics/Plays 308

The Light of Asia *by sir Edwin Arnold*   ISBN: *1-59462-204-3* **$13.95**
In this poetic masterpiece, Edwin Arnold describes the life and teachings of Buddha. The man who was to become known as Buddha to the world was born as Prince Gautama of India but he rejected the worldly riches and abandoned the reigns of power when...
Religion/History/Biographies Pages 170

The Complete Works of Guy de Maupassant *by Guy de Maupassant*   ISBN: *1-59462-157-8* **$16.95**
"For days and days, nights and nights, I had dreamed of that first kiss which was to consecrate our engagement, and I knew not on what spot I should put my lips..."
Fiction/Classics Pages 240

The Art of Cross-Examination *by Francis L. Wellman*   ISBN: *1-59462-309-0* **$26.95**
Written by a renowned trial lawyer, Wellman imparts his experience and uses case studies to explain how to use psychology to extract desired information through questioning.
How-to/Science/Reference Pages 408

Answered or Unanswered? *by Louisa Vaughan*   ISBN: *1-59462-248-5* **$10.95**
Miracles of Faith in China
Religion Pages 112

The Edinburgh Lectures on Mental Science (1909) *by Thomas*   ISBN: *1-59462-008-3* **$11.95**
This book contains the substance of a course of lectures recently given by the writer in the Queen Street Hall, Edinburgh. Its purpose is to indicate the Natural Principles governing the relation between Mental Action and Material Conditions...
New Age/Psychology Pages 148

Ayesha *by H. Rider Haggard*   ISBN: *1-59462-301-5* **$24.95**
Verily and indeed it is the unexpected that happens! Probably if there was one person upon the earth from whom the Editor of this, and of a certain previous history, did not expect to hear again...
Classics Pages 380

Ayala's Angel *by Anthony Trollope*   ISBN: *1-59462-352-X* **$29.95**
The two girls were both pretty, but Lucy who was twenty-one who supposed to be simple and comparatively unattractive, whereas Ayala was credited, as her Bombwhat romantic name might show, with poetic charm and a taste for romance. Ayala when her father died was nineteen...
Fiction Pages 484

The American Commonwealth *by James Bryce*   ISBN: *1-59462-286-8* **$34.45**
An interpretation of American democratic political theory. It examines political mechanics and society from the perspective of Scotsman James Bryce
Politics Pages 572

Stories of the Pilgrims *by Margaret P. Pumphrey*   ISBN: *1-59462-116-0* **$17.95**
This book explores pilgrims religious oppression in England as well as their escape to Holland and eventual crossing to America on the Mayflower, and their early days in New England...
History Pages 268

QTY

The Fasting Cure *by Sinclair Upton* ISBN: *1-59462-222-1* **$13.95**
In the Cosmopolitan Magazine for May, 1910, and in the Contemporary Review (London) for April, 1910, I published an article dealing with my experiences in fasting. I have written a great many magazine articles, but never one which attracted so much attention... New Age/Self Help/Health Pages 164

Hebrew Astrology *by Sepharial* ISBN: *1-59462-308-2* **$13.45**
In these days of advanced thinking it is a matter of common observation that we have left many of the old landmarks behind and that we are now pressing forward to greater heights and to a wider horizon than that which represented the mind-content of our progenitors... Astrology Pages 144

Thought Vibration or The Law of Attraction in the Thought World ISBN: *1-59462-127-6* **$12.95**

by William Walker Atkinson *Psychology/Religion Pages 144*

Optimism *by Helen Keller* ISBN: *1-59462-108-X* **$15.95**
Helen Keller was blind, deaf, and mute since 19 months old, yet famously learned how to overcome these handicaps, communicate with the world, and spread her lectures promoting optimism. An inspiring read for everyone... Biographies/Inspirational Pages 84

Sara Crewe *by Frances Burnett* ISBN: *1-59462-360-0* **$9.45**
In the first place, Miss Minchin lived in London. Her home was a large, dull, tall one, in a large, dull square, where all the houses were alike, and all the sparrows were alike, and where all the door-knockers made the same heavy sound... Childrens/Classic Pages 88

The Autobiography of Benjamin Franklin *by Benjamin Franklin* ISBN: *1-59462-135-7* **$24.95**
The Autobiography of Benjamin Franklin has probably been more extensively read than any other American historical work, and no other book of its kind has had such ups and downs of fortune. Franklin lived for many years in England, where he was agent... Biographies/History Pages 332

Name	
Email	
Telephone	
Address	
City, State ZIP	

☐ **Credit Card**   ☐ **Check / Money Order**

Credit Card Number	
Expiration Date	
Signature	

Please Mail to: Book Jungle
                        PO Box 2226
                        Champaign, IL 61825
or Fax to: 630-214-0564

ORDERING INFORMATION

web: *www.bookjungle.com*
email: *sales@bookjungle.com*
fax: *630-214-0564*
mail: *Book Jungle PO Box 2226 Champaign, IL 61825*
or PayPal *to sales@bookjungle.com*

Please contact us for bulk discounts

DIRECT-ORDER TERMS

**20% Discount if You Order
Two or More Books**
Free Domestic Shipping!
Accepted: Master Card, Visa,
Discover, American Express

www.ingramcontent.com/pod-product-compliance
Lightning Source LLC
Chambersburg PA
CBHW080507110426
42742CB00017B/3025

* 9 7 8 1 4 3 8 5 3 4 9 6 1 *